Take This Job & Love It

Solving the Problems You Face at Work

With Study Questions for Individuals or Groups

STANLEY C. BALDWIN

INTERVARSITY PRESS
DOWNERS GROVE, ILLINOIS 60515

InterVarsity Press is the book-publishing division of InterVarsity Christian Fellowship, a student movement active on campus at hundreds of universities, colleges and schools of nursing. For information about local and regional activities, write Public Relations Dept., InterVarsity Christian Fellowship, 6400 Schroeder Rd., P.O. Box 7895, Madison, WI 53707-7895.

Distributed in Canada through InterVarsity Press, 860 Denison St., Unit 3, Markham, Ontario L3R 4H1, Canada.

All Scripture quotations, unless otherwise indicated, are from the Holy Bible, New International Version. Copyright © 1973, 1978, International Bible Society. Used by permission of Zondervan Bible Publishers.

Cover illustration: Guy Wolek

ISBN 0-8308-1250-4

Printed in the United States of America

Library of Congress Cataloging in Publication Data

Baldwin, Stanley C.
  Take this job and love it : solving the problems you face at work
  Stanley C. Baldwin.
    p. cm.
  Bibliography: p.
  ISBN 0-8308-1250-4
  1. Work—Religious aspects—Christianity.   2. Job satisfaction.
3. Christian life—1960-   I. Title.
BT738.5.B35 1988
248.8'8—dc19   88-12839
CIP

17	16	15	14	13	12	11	10	9	8	7	6	5	4	3	2	1
99	98	97	96	95	94	93	92	91	90	89	88					

*To
Lloyd Cory,
my former boss,
who not only encouraged me
to write this book
but also passed along
to me the fruits
of his own research*

1

Serving God in the Workplace

· · · · · · · ·

*T*o me it was incredible.

A large group of us from church had taken an entire evening to travel from the suburbs into the city and sit in a studio for over three hours—all to provide a live audience for our pastor's TV program. Every couple of weeks church leaders encouraged the congregation to "do something great for God" by being a part of this TV audience.

I came away from the experience shaking my head. I certainly didn't feel I had done anything great for God. Maybe the presence of a live audience helped our pastor preach a little better, but it required a considerable time and effort on the part of many people for what seemed to me a small gain.

What emptiness, I thought, must characterize people's everyday lives if attending a TV taping qualifies as "doing something great for God"!

My ungreat TV experience prompted me to think more deeply about the attitudes Christians take toward the work that fills their days. Work seems to provide so little sense of spiritual fulfillment that many Christians will grasp at anything (even sitting in a TV audience) if it counts as doing something for God. What about the forty hours a week, two thousand hours a year, ninety thousand hours a lifetime that the average person spends in the workplace? Is that time spiritually meaningless?

A Biblical View of Work

The Bible speaks directly to these questions: "Whatever you do, work at it with all your heart, as working for the Lord, not for men, since you know that you will receive an inheritance from the Lord as a reward. It is the Lord Christ you are serving" (Col 3:23-24; see also Eph 6:7-8).

This passage clearly states that any kind of work, done as to the Lord, is accepted by him and will be rewarded accordingly. The context of these words makes their message even stronger because they were originally directed to slaves (see v. 22). Even *involuntary* work for earthly masters counts as service to God. Why, then, do so many people think that only what they do under the auspices of the church has divine significance?

This text not only tells us *how* we should view our work, but *why* we should view it that way:

How: "As working for the Lord."

Why: "It is the Lord Christ you are serving."

Viewing our work as being for the Lord, then, is not just a nice, spiritual attitude to have. Scripture doesn't say, "You really may be working for a miserable slave master in a dreary and demeaning task, but it will help if you take a positive attitude." No. We should consider our work as being for the Lord *because it is.*

Adam Gets a Job

Let's go back to the very beginning. The story is a familiar one. "In the beginning God created . . ." (Gen 1:1). We see God himself at work creating the heavens and the earth, all creatures great and small, and man and woman. Seven times during this account in Genesis 1, Scripture emphasizes that God was pleased with his labor ("God saw that it was good"), even though his work was not directly "spiritual" in nature. As if to emphasize the work involved in creating the world, the second chapter of Genesis begins with God resting (though I'm sure he was not tired): "By the seventh day God had finished the work he had been doing; so on the seventh day he rested from all his work" (2:2).

The story continues. God took the man he had created, placed him in a garden paradise and said, "Now, just enjoy it." Right?

Not quite. Let's check the record.

"The Lord God took the man and put him in the Garden of Eden to work it and take care of it" (Gen 2:15). Here at the very dawn of time, before sin ever entered into human experience, man was given work to do. In other words, Adam had a job. He was to care for a garden that had been planted by God himself (see v. 8).

God could have made a garden that required no tending. He could have created a changeless plastic paradise. Instead he made plants that needed to be nurtured, trimmed, trained and controlled. Clearly, *part of God's original design was for us to*

11

work. Therefore, when we work, we are following God's plan.

Some believe the false notion that work is a curse. They fail to understand that the command to work was not only implicit in those first instructions about tending the garden, but also in God's command to subdue the whole earth and take dominion over it (see Gen 1:28).

Now it is true that the nature of work was affected by the curse. After Adam sinned, God said: "Cursed is the ground because of you; through painful toil you will eat of it all the days of your life. It will produce thorns and thistles for you, and you will eat the plants of the field. By the sweat of your brow you will eat your food until you return to the ground, since from it you were taken; for dust you are and to dust you will return" (Gen 3:17-19).

This passage does not say that work itself is a part of the curse. Rather, it indicates that work would become "painful"— that, like the ground, work would now be flawed or marred. The ground would bring forth thistles and thorns, as well as the edible and delightful plants it previously produced. Work would include elements of fatigue, frustration and desperation, as well as the fulfillment it previously offered. Nevertheless, work itself remained a good thing, an essential element in an arrangement that God pronounced good and very good.

Of course, you and I live a long way from Eden. Countless seasons have passed over the earth's gardens, and we are many generations removed from our first parents. Technology has given us complicated tools to replace the spade and the hoe. Many of us work in concrete and asphalt cities away from the soil and the sun and the sod. We report to supervisors who in turn report to others up a long ladder.

Living so far from Eden, we easily forget that all creation is

God's garden. He has placed us here to take care of things for him, and when we work (no matter where it is in God's great garden) we serve the Lord. The pay we get, the system under which we operate, the kindness or orneriness of our boss—those are incidentals. Not that they are unimportant; in fact, much of this book deals with those "incidentals" of the workplace. But the basic principle we must establish is that when we work, we serve Christ our Lord.

What Difference Does It Make?

This one basic principle—that our work serves God—has staggering implications. For one, it means we don't have to waste that ninety thousand hours we spend on the job. They count for eternity!

The fact that we work for God also means that we need never be truly "unemployed." Though at various times in our lives we may be out of a job that pays the bills, God presents us with opportunities every day to help take care of his creation—whether it's spending time with the elderly, tutoring children with learning disabilities or keeping the house clean for other "working" members of the family. Of course, you need a way to put food on the table and keep a roof over your head. But even while you are out of an economically rewarding job, serving God in other ways can still lift your spirits and preserve your self-respect.

Working for God not only assures us of "employment" but of compensation as well. Few things take the steam out of us like feeling that our efforts are not appreciated or that we are being exploited on the job. Workers slough off, even sabotage the projects on which they are employed, when they sense that they are not being treated right.

Because God is just and righteous, you cannot do good work in God's garden and not get paid: "God is not unjust; he will not forget your work and the love you have shown him as you have helped his people and continue to help them" (Heb 6:10). While this verse speaks directly about work done on behalf of Christian brothers and sisters, the principle applies more broadly. Paul makes it clear in Colossians 3:23-24 that any good work we do, no matter what the circumstance, serves God and will be rewarded by God.

This principle helped me recently when I "lost" more than three months of diligent labor. I owned a run-down rental house that also suffered from some design problems. A "balloon payment" was soon coming due, and I knew I couldn't afford to pay it. I would either have to sell the house or let it go back to the previous owner.

I thought that if I fixed up the house, it would sell. Still, fixing it was a risk: if it didn't sell, I would never recoup all the work and expense of remodeling. What to do?

I decided that fixing up the house had merit in and of itself, regardless of how I came out on the deal. Some family would be living in that house. Would they have an ugly bathroom with no shower, an old tub and a water-damaged floor? Or would they enjoy a newly-designed tub and shower with nicely tiled walls and floor? Would they have a dark and damp back bedroom with two little postage-stamp sized windows? Or would they have, on one wall, large and stylish double-glazed windows, looking out on a private back yard?

I not only renovated the bedroom and bath, but added electrical outlets, painted and papered other rooms, laid new carpet, and improved the outside drainage.

The house didn't sell. I had to let it go back. I lost all that

14

money and time since I did the work myself.

It was, I suppose, a poor business decision. I certainly would have preferred to sell it at a profit. However, I do not consider my work lost. Apart from the biblical principles that affirm the inherent value of work, I probably would. But I believe God. I dressed up a section of his garden, and I have no doubt that God will take care of my proper reward. "The Lord will reward everyone for whatever good he does" (Eph 6:8).

Is Secular Work Second-Rate?

The church has not ignored the message of Scripture about the dignity of work. Many fine sermons have been preached on the very passage in Colossians which I cited earlier. Faithful to that text, preachers proclaim that we are to do our work heartily as unto the Lord and that he will reward such service.

Unfortunately, the church has also communicated the impression that secular work is second-rate. When not actually addressing the subject of work (which is most of the time), preachers tend to contradict the scriptural view, even if not directly. Too often they communicate that working in the marketplace serves God, but that working directly for the church *SERVES GOD.*

I heard one good pastor tell his congregation, "All of us have different gifts to use in the service of Christ. Some can teach, some can sing, some can hold church office and some can work in the business world earning money to support the work of Christ"—as if business had no validity in and of itself.

The result? A double message goes forth, with preachers saying one thing when addressing the subject of work directly and quite another the rest of the time.

I don't mean to say that sitting in on a pastor's TV show so he'll have a live audience doesn't serve God. God looks on our

15

hearts, and anything we do out of love for the Lord has value. But when church leaders constantly emphasize that only church-related activities qualify as great service to God, they imply that secular work is something less. I will develop these ideas further in the next two chapters.

Trouble in the Workplace

In singing the praises of work and calling it first-class service to God, I feel a little like I did when I used to tell our kids that liver and broccoli are good for you. It was hard for me to be convincing when they were gagging.

People in difficult work situations find the work-is-wonderful idea similarly hard to swallow. Many single women in today's work force are trying to maintain a home while they work long hours outside the home for low wages. Despite all their efforts, they cannot afford decent housing, food and medical care for their families. More and more men are also a part of the working poor. They hold full-time jobs, but they still are not able to make ends meet.

Just as the working poor may well gag on my work-is-wonderful advice, so might those who feel trapped in jobs that are demeaning or physically harmful.

Tell the asbestos worker dying of cancer that his job was a loving provision from an all-wise God, and he might be entitled to doubt you. Far too many other workers have also been poisoned on the job by toxic substances, sickened by radiation, maimed by machines, sexually harassed or discriminated against by coworkers, or subjected to destructive levels of stress.

People working at jobs that trade off their well-being for production don't always have good alternatives. Another job may be difficult to find.

16

Practical Problem-Solving

Like everyone else, Christians face various work-related difficulties:

☐ the work involves wrong or questionable practices

☐ the boss is incompetent or unreasonable

☐ the employer is unfair

☐ coworkers are obnoxious or difficult

☐ the job is boring

☐ the work environment puts health at risk

☐ the job involves considerable stress

In chapters four through ten I will address these practical issues. Then, in chapter eleven, I will explore the pitfalls of letting work become an idol. Finally, I will devote the last chapter to the question of changing careers. Many people do change careers at some point during their work life, and many more wonder whether or not they should. We will discuss some of the principles involved as well as the practical implications.

Throughout the book I will seek to be down-to-earth and practical. I do not write for scholars or theorists. My purpose is not simply to help people be informed about the workplace, but to help them function as Christians in it.

My credentials? Well, I have worked as:

a newspaper carrier

a candy vendor (my own business)

a used car dealer

a retail clerk

a soda jerk

a restaurant dishwasher

a delivery man

a toy-airplane factory worker

a maintenance machinist in heavy industry

17

a manager of an agricultural chemical plant
a gyroscope machine technician
a truck-fleet mechanic
a frozen-food warehouse worker
a carpenter's helper
a roofer
a plywood mill worker
a school-bus driver
a substitute high-school teacher
a land developer
a pastor
an editor
and a writer

Some of the jobs I held during my youth, to pay expenses while in school. Other jobs filled in gaps between "good" jobs. Whatever the case, I have been out there in the trenches. I have worked blue-collar jobs, white-collar jobs and as a professional.

And what do I hope to accomplish through this book? Actually, something quite wonderful.

You see, I suspect that, like me, you want your life to count for something. You want to please and glorify God. So why write off the biggest single chunk of your life? You no doubt spend more of your waking hours at work than at anything else. Far more. For every hour you can spend teaching the Bible, singing in the choir, or serving in church work, you probably spend ten hours on the job. Wouldn't it be great if you could capture all of those work hours—two thousand of them every year—for God?

I believe you can.

In fact, I am certain of it.

For Individuals or Groups

1. What are some positive work experiences you have had? What made them enjoyable for you?

2. What bad work experiences have you had? What made them so troublesome?

3. Why do you think God included work as part of his original design for us, something he built in even before the Fall in Genesis 3 (pp. 11-13)?

4. Do you think the church values work outside a Christian setting (pp. 15-16)? Explain.

5. Do you feel like "secular" work has the same value in God's eyes as "spiritual" work? Why or why not?

6. On page 16 it says, "In singing the praises of work and calling it first-class service to God, I feel a little like I did when I used to tell our kids that liver and broccoli are good for you. It was hard for me to be convincing when they were gagging." Is the idea of work as first-class service hard for you to swallow? Why or why not?

2

Can I Best Glorify God in Full-Time Christian Work?

·········

*M*any Christians feel spiritually unfulfilled. They yearn to obey the words of Jesus, "Do not work for food that spoils, but for food that endures to eternal life" (Jn 6:27). They want to serve God, but they are stuck. They have to make a living, and their job drains away most of their time and energy. So they feel dissatisfied, even guilty.

I understand this feeling because I struggle with it myself. I write and speak on spiritual themes. This work fulfills me. However, I also work a good deal with my hands. This spring I have extensively redecorated our house and done a lot of yard work.

I realize that my work around the house is not exactly like having an eight-hour-a-day job, but I've been in that situation for many years too. Even when I have enjoyed my jobs, I have sometimes felt frustrated and confused that my work seems unrelated to my spirituality.

Recently I spent all day rooting out weeds from our flower beds. "This is kind of a waste," I told my wife Marge. "Next spring you won't be able to tell I did any of this work. I'll need to do it all again."

"Tell me about it!" she replied. "Most of my life has been like that."

I knew what she was talking about. I used to thank God I was not saddled with endless cleaning and cooking chores, never seeming to get anywhere. When facing some mundane task I have thought, Am I supposed to expend my time and energy on cleaning (or whatever) when I could be writing about or preaching the gospel? I understand how easy it is to buy into the notion that certain kinds of work (such as preaching, teaching, witnessing) are *SERVING GOD,* while other kinds of work (such as weeding and cleaning) are, at best, serving God.

If our secular jobs leave us feeling spiritually unfulfilled, we have several options:

1. We can leave our jobs to concentrate on full-time Christian service.

2. We can keep our unfulfilling jobs but compensate by getting more involved in Christian activities.

3. We can learn to glorify God in our secular work.

We can also, of course, accept defeat and go on as we have been. But that's unnecessary. Let's consider our other three options one by one.

Seeking a Full-time Christian Vocation
Dissatisfaction with a secular job could be an early indicator that

you should go into the ministry. Certainly God does call people from secular to "spiritual" occupations. Andrew, Peter, James and John were fishermen until Jesus called them to become "fishers of men" (Mt 4:19). Making a career change in midlife is not uncommon these days, and significant numbers of people are leaving secular jobs to go into ministry.

Within the past few weeks I have encountered two men who in midlife decided to prepare for the pastorate. One has succeeded; the other has not. The one who succeeded is a better pastor for his time spent in the secular workplace. The other man has been unable to find a pastorate, and it now appears that he never will. He preaches poorly, is not particularly personable and faces bleak prospects for the future.

This man denied himself and his family a great deal to pursue his dream, the lowered standard of living they endured during his seminary days being the least of it. In many ways he demanded a greater sacrifice of his family than he did of himself. His wife and children were uprooted from their home and stripped of the security of his steady job.

Obviously, you need to think long and hard before chucking a secular job in favor of the ministry.

Unfulfilled Preachers

Even those who successfully switch from secular to Christian work are not guaranteed a fulfilling life of spiritual service by virtue of their positions. You probably would not believe how many Christian workers think about leaving the ministry.

A 1978 Gallup poll asked both Protestant and Catholic clergy whether and with what frequency they considered leaving the ministry. Only twenty-nine per cent of all those polled said they never considered seeking some other kind of work. In other

23

words, about seven out of every ten ministers polled thought about quitting. In the 30-49 age bracket, it was even worse: only twenty-one per cent said they never considered leaving. This poll focused on individuals who were still in the ministry at the time; disaffected ministers who had already left were not included.

In fairness, the same poll indicated that another forty-one per cent of all ministers seldom considered leaving, so not all who sometimes waver feel deeply dissatisfied. Still, some ministers are just sticking it out until retirement because they have no other decent job prospects. These people don't brim over with a sense of spiritual fulfillment, even though their whole job supposedly serves God.

The Allure of Christian Work

Full-time ministry carries a certain mystique that we need to understand. When you see some of the reasons that full-time ministry attracts people, you not only safeguard yourself against going into it for the wrong reasons, but also better equip yourself to find satisfaction in secular work.

First, full-time ministry may appeal to the ego. The very structure of most churches elevates the full-time Christian worker. Who stands in the limelight at church? Who gets the attention and dominates the platform? The pastor, naturally.

As a bank president, schoolteacher or lawyer, you may have status in the community, but in the church you are usually a member of the supporting cast. The minister is the star. The only person who might outshine the minister is the full-time worker who has gained even greater prominence. In some churches that might be an evangelist, a missionary, a denominational executive or a celebrity such as a musician, TV personality or author.

When asked what he wanted to be when he grew up, one boy replied without hesitation, "A missionary—home on furlough." He didn't relish living in a foreign country, but he certainly liked the idea of traveling around telling admirers of his exploits.

Similarly, I know of a recently converted nightclub performer who set his sights on the ministry. He enjoyed being center stage, working an audience, producing certain feelings and reactions. Not impressed with the performances of the pastors he had heard, he thought he could preach as well as most of them. "Actually," he confided, "I could do it better!" His "call" to preach at that point was mostly just an ego trip, a desire for prominence.

We must not be lured by the prestige of the ministry into thinking that it is the only or best way for us to serve God.

Christians sometimes feel dissatisfied in their jobs partly because they hear the strong if unspoken message that God thinks secular work is second-rate. "Our pastor was so happy because both of his children had answered the call to full-time Christian ministry," one woman recently told me. "He acted as if any other choice on their part would be something akin to their being caught using drugs or having babies out of wedlock. While he was talking, I couldn't help but wonder, Is the ministry so much greater than any other work? What does that make me as a clerk-typist—chopped liver?"

Needed: A Call

Make no mistake: full-time Christian work is a high and holy calling. However, it is not one that a person should choose lightly. The Bible teaches that one needs a call to leave the secular workplace in favor of full-time Christian service.

Some argue otherwise. I speak as one thoroughly familiar

with their stance. I received my Bible training at a school renowned for turning out foreign missionaries. While I was studying there, a common belief (though not the official teaching of the school) was that you do not need a special call to undertake missionary work. We have the command of Jesus: "Go ye into all the world, and preach the gospel to every creature" (Mk 16:15 KJV). Our duty, some of us thought, is to obey that command. The vocational choice that requires a special call is taking a job that keeps you at home.

Though I avidly supported that view at the time, my wife Marge didn't see things the same way. After our fourth child was born and our second-oldest experienced life-threatening reactions to the inoculations needed for foreign service, Marge began dragging her feet about going to the Third World. I felt as if my life were being ruined. To me, spiritual fulfillment meant becoming a missionary in an impoverished country.

I have since come to understand that Scripture teaches us not to enter into a ministry vocation just because we follow Christ. The Bible is specific about this:

Each one should remain in the situation which he was in when God called him. Were you a slave when you were called? Don't let it trouble you—although if you can gain your freedom, do so. For he who was a slave when he was called by the Lord is the Lord's freedman; similarly, he who was a free man when he was called is Christ's slave. You were bought at a price; do not become slaves of men. Brothers, each man, as responsible to God, should remain in the situation God called him to. (1 Cor 7:20-24)

Notice that this passage begins and ends with the words "remain in the situation." The larger context mentions several kinds of situations that one should not automatically try to change on the basis of becoming a believer in Christ. One does not change marital status in order to follow Christ (vv. 12-17). One does not seek to become circumcised or uncircumcised (vv. 17-20). And one does not necessarily change vocation, even if one's vocation is that of a slave (vv. 20-24).

Throughout the passage, the continuing refrain (heard no less than three times) tells us to stay put unless compelling reasons other than simply becoming a Christian encourage us to seek a change. Furthermore, Paul declares, "This is the rule I lay down in all the churches" (v. 17). In other words, the "stay put" admonition is not an exceptional or occasional command but a general principle.

Paul undoubtedly had as great a missionary heart as anyone who ever lived. However, he was also specifically called to his work for God (see Acts 13:2-3). He did not try to press others into his mold. Instead of recruiting everyone he possibly could for missionary work, Paul told his converts to stay with the vocation they were in when grace found them.

Putting Church Work in Perspective

At the beginning of the chapter, I suggested that Christians who feel spiritually unfulfilled in a secular job might consider becoming more involved in Christian work after hours.

Certainly the church provides opportunities for meaningful Christian service. We can teach, sing, play an instrument, visit the sick or imprisoned, bring food to the hungry, usher, tend the nursery, care for church property—the list goes on and on. Every church needs lay people to carry out its ministry. Pastors and other full-time Christian workers can't do it all.

Still, we make a mistake when we let an unfulfilling job motivate us to get more involved in church work. First, we leave

27

the problem unresolved. Our work remains a spiritual wasteland. Second, we commit ourselves to Christian work for the wrong reasons. There are many good reasons to be active in the work of the church. Work because the church needs your gifts, because you enjoy serving others and, above all, because you love God. But working in the church to compensate for serious deficiencies in your vocational life may pave the way for burnout. I suspect that many people, driven by the need to "do something great for God" outside their forty-hour work week, overcommit themselves. Some end up changing churches or dropping out altogether, just to free themselves of the burden.

A Question of Obedience

In our minds we must reconcile biblical commands to earn our own bread with Jesus' admonition not to work for the bread that perishes, but for that which endures forever (see 2 Thess 3:6-12; Jn 6:27).

Clearly, we are to seek first God's kingdom and his righteousness. Food and drink and clothing are the incidentals of life, not its aim. But we still need to earn a living, and Paul admonishes us to work to support ourselves. Anyone departing from this standard must be called of God to be an exception to the rule.

Your first step toward making your vocation glorifying to God, then, is to realize that in working you are obeying his will. Obedience is always the critical issue. As Samuel said, "Does the Lord delight in burnt offerings and sacrifices as much as in obeying the voice of the Lord? To obey is better than sacrifice, and to heed is better than the fat of rams" (1 Sam 15:22).

Do not imagine that God would be pleased with you if you sacrificed yourself on the altar of full-time Christian ministry. Unless God has called you to such service, he has already made known his will: "Work with your hands . . . so that your daily life may win the respect of outsiders and so that you will not be dependent on anybody" (1 Thess 4:11-12).

If you are doing this, rejoice. Do not let your adversary the devil trouble you with accusations that you aren't doing anything for God. You are doing exactly what he commands.

Believing that you work for God will make any work you do spiritually fulfilling. What kind of work you do pales in importance to whether or not you do work in obedience to God. Writing about Francis of Assisi, the eminent church historian Augustus Neander said, "He constantly taught that a heart fixed on God is all that gives actions their real importance."[1] Thus Francis could preach to the masses or to the birds and do so with equal fervor. Whatever he did was for God.

I don't think that most of us could preach to the birds with much fervor; but for us, that would not be an act of obedience to God. That is the key.

In the next chapter we'll use this key of obedience to unlock the secret of glorifying God in secular work.

For Individuals or Groups

1. On a scale of 1 (low) to 10 (high), how would you rate the spiritual level of satisfaction you have with your current job? Explain.

2. Why is full-time Christian work alluring to many Christians? How alluring is it to you?

3. On page 25 it says, "One needs a call to leave the secular workplace in favor of full-time Christian service." How would you define a *call?* Do you agree that a call is needed to change jobs like this?

4. Why is it not always right to enter into a ministry vocation (pp. 26-27)?

5. What are the pluses and minuses of becoming more involved in Christian work after hours to fulfill us spiritually (pp. 27-28)?

6. How can we balance the biblical commands to earn our bread with Jesus' admonition to work not for the bread that perishes but that endures (see 2 Thess 3:6-12 and Jn 6:27, p. 28)?

3

How Can I Glorify God in Secular Work?

· · · · · · · ·

*C*harles *"Buzzy" Morgan had it made. After finishing* college, he had landed a good position with a major department store in Seattle. However, some of us who knew Buzzy felt uneasy about his success. A highly motivated college graduate bent on climbing the corporate ladder, Buzzy had resisted Christianity for years. Now that his career had taken off, we wondered if he would ever see his need for Christ.

Not too long afterward came the surprising news: Buzzy had become a Christian! Achieving the career goal he had worked for so long left him feeling empty, he said. He realized that there had to be more to life. Buzzy turned wholeheartedly to Christ, committed his life to God's service and soon entered seminary to prepare for the ministry.

The Reverend Charles Morgan's first church was located in the small town of Marion, Oregon, not far from where I lived. His ministry was fruitful. He moved from there to a bigger church in Seattle and then to Portland.

Sometime afterward I heard that Charles had left the ministry, but I knew no details. Years later, as I began research for this book, I wanted to interview someone who had left the ministry to pursue secular work. My friend Roger Smith, who had left the pastorate but stayed in Christian ministry, gave me a lead. "My predecessor at the last church I pastored runs a janitorial business now. We have kept in touch over the years, and I'd say he does pretty well at working to the glory of God. You should talk with him. His name is Charles Morgan."

Cleaning Floors to God's Glory

Could this really be Charles Morgan? I wondered. I called the phone number Roger gave me. It was Buzzy all right. He was glad to hear from me and readily agreed to an interview.

At the appointed time, we sat down and began to talk. "I know that Colossians 3:23-24 says we are supposed to do our work, whatever it is, as unto the Lord," I said. "And if we do that, the Lord accepts it as service to him. I grasp that intellectually, but I don't always feel that way about it emotionally. Have you been able to integrate that principle into your life?"

Yes, Buzzy believed that he was cleaning floors and performing other janitorial services to the glory of God. I pressed him for details, wondering if he would offer the usual consolations: "I sometimes have opportunity to witness"; "I can support the work of God financially with my earnings"; "I clean the floors of churches and other Christian organizations."

Buzzy did not say any of those things.

"It's attitude," he told me.

"Okay," I said, "and what is your attitude while you are down there cleaning somebody's dirty floors?"

Buzzy looked me straight in the eye. "What's my attitude, day by day on the job? It's 'Thank you, Lord; thank you that I am doing just exactly what you want me to do.' "

"We are called to obedience," he continued, "whatever that involves. We only need to listen to God and do his will. It doesn't matter what the job is so long as we are doing his will. That is what glorifies God."

"But how do you know you're doing God's will?" I asked.

"We need to cultivate a listening ear so we will know his will," Buzzy said. "I believe we can absolutely depend on God to lead us if we are listening. I take this matter of listening to God very seriously. Every day I read my Bible, pray and keep a journal of what's happening in my spiritual life. The journal is important. It helps keep me accountable."

"Do you think you will ever go back into the pastoral ministry?" I asked.

"Possibly," said Buzzy. "I'm open to it. But obedience—that's the main thing."

Delighting God

Again we come to a profound Old Testament question: "Does the LORD delight in burnt offerings and sacrifices as much as in obeying the voice of the LORD?" (1 Sam 15:22). Samuel spoke those words to King Saul, who, after slaying the Amalekites, had spared some of their sheep and cattle, which the Lord had directed him to destroy.

Saul claimed he had good reason to save the animals—"in

33

order to sacrifice them to the LORD" (v. 21). But Samuel didn't buy Saul's excuse. In answer to his own question about what delights the Lord, the prophet said, "To obey is better than sacrifice, and to heed is better than the fat of rams" (v. 22).

God spoke a similar message to Israel through the prophet Jeremiah: "For when I brought your forefathers out of Egypt and spoke to them, I did not just give them commands about burnt offerings and sacrifices, but I gave them this command: 'Obey me, and I will be your God and you will be my people' " (Jer 7:22-23).

The Lord wants obedience from us, not sacrifice. Our work may not carry any directly "Christian" responsibilities or be recognized by others as service to God. It may not even feel important. But if it represents faithful obedience to God on our part, God delights in it.

When we obey God in our work, we witness to the entire spiritual universe—to angels, to demons, and to man—that, like Jesus, we embrace the will of the Father. Talk about being a witness on the job!

Keeping the Balance

Work is not the only arena in which God calls for our obedience, of course. God also calls us to obey him in worship. Remember the opening chapters of Genesis: God placed man in the Garden of Eden to work and keep it, but God also came in the cool of the day to fellowship with Adam and receive his worship. Similarly, God also calls us to obey him by witnessing to others: "You will be my witnesses . . . to the ends of the earth" (Acts 1:8).

Today, we can find much fulfillment in a life of obedient work, worship and witness. In our fallen world, however, work, worship and witness may seem to compete for our time rather than complement one another. We often tend to exalt one of these activities at the expense of the others, as if one were serving God and the others were inferior.

This kind of thinking must have influenced the employee who told store owner Deanie Ferguson that his priority at work wasn't to fulfill his duties, but to witness for Christ. As a committed Christian, Deanie cares about witnessing too—but believes that all employees ought to do their jobs first of all. She also believes that slacking off on the job does not make a good witness.

But, you might ask, didn't Jesus say that spiritual matters are more important than work? Once Jesus visited the home of Mary and Martha. When Martha (who was busy serving Jesus in the kitchen) complained that Mary (who was sitting at Jesus' feet) wasn't helping her, Jesus defended Mary: "Mary has chosen what is better, and it will not be taken away from her" (Lk 10:42).

We misinterpret this passage when we imagine that it exalts worship and denigrates work. If worship is always "better" than work, we should worship all the time and not work at all. Clearly that's not what God intends. Rather, Jesus is saying that Martha was working when she should have been worshiping.

We still have many Marthas with us today. They not only work—they are workaholics. They try to find all their meaning and purpose for life in their vocations. They have no time to witness or worship. (We'll explore this problem further in chapter 11.)

For now, our point is simply that God wants us to obey him: to work wholeheartedly when we should work, to worship gladly when we should worship, and to witness when he provides the opportunity, on or off the job.

35

Working in obedience to God infuses our jobs with meaning. But work glorifies God in ways besides being an act of obedience. Let's look at some.

Serving Others Glorifies God

My early Christian life was strongly influenced by a couplet:

Only one life, 'twill soon be past

Only what's done for Christ will last.

I interpreted that to mean secular work had no spiritual or eternal value. Again, that idea was reinforced by Christian leaders, whether they actually intended to do so or not. Consider, for example, the story of one Christian man who turned away from a civil engineering career to do something of value:

My objective—to be a civil engineer and build bridges, dams, and roads, lasted until I came across 2 Peter 3:10. What a shock, then to realize that everything I planned to build, God would come along and destroy!

. . . So I prayed, "God, I don't want to give my life to nothing. Why pour 70 years into something and then discover you will burn it and leave me empty-handed?"[1]

I was, therefore, deeply troubled when at one point in my life some doors of opportunity for Christian service closed to me. I was grieving about this one night, sleeping only fitfully. Toward morning, my mind settled on Jesus' words: "I tell you the truth, whatever you did for one of the least of these brothers of mine, you did for me" (Mt 25:40).

The Holy Spirit seemed to be reassuring me that I could still serve Jesus in a significant way, even if certain doors had closed. Maybe I couldn't stand on a platform and "minister," but I could certainly serve somebody in Jesus' name.

The next day I said, "Well, today I am going to go help Jesus install new counter tops on his kitchen cabinets." I knew a brother in Christ who was needing help with that task, and I decided to take Jesus at his word.

I can't say I felt any special glow as I worked that day. The job had its standard quota of difficulties and frustrations. But I did it for Jesus, and in that I rejoiced. I felt a new sense of peace as I realized that no one can prevent me from ministering, because the word minister simply means to serve. If I never stand in a pulpit, if I never teach a Bible class, if I never hold a position in "Christian work," Jesus says he will accept what I do for the least of his brothers as being done for him.

Scripture also teaches us to serve people whether we consider them to be Christian brothers and sisters or not: "Therefore, as we have opportunity, let us do good to all people, especially to those who belong to the family of believers" (Gal 6:10).

So serving people serves Jesus. That's good news to those in secular work, because most jobs involve serving others. After all, who would be willing to pay for someone to do work that wasn't providing a valuable service?

Of course, some jobs render more disservice to others than service. A drug dealer "serves" the user by supplying drugs, but this clearly does not serve the user's (and society's) best interests. The pornography, tobacco and arms industries represent other fields where workers could have trouble serving humanity well.

While most employees render a service, however, some do so cheerfully and others do so grudgingly. If you're working only for the wages or your own advancement, you're probably rendering a service halfheartedly—and not glorifying God as you might.

A schoolteacher with a serving spirit, for example, can make

37

a tremendous difference. My granddaughter Heidi was fortunate enough to have Miss Giannetti as her fourth-grade teacher. Miss Giannetti was a Christian who obviously cared about her students. She didn't simply teach fourth grade; she tried to serve her students by responding to their individual talents and needs.

Miss Giannetti told Heidi's mother that Heidi wrote well and should be encouraged to develop her skills. She also came on her own time to attend Heidi's piano recital. Miss Giannetti noticed that another child was a poor reader. Although she could not take the time from the rest of the class to give that child the personal help he needed, she recruited a volunteer teacher's aide to tutor him.

Miss Giannetti reminds me of the fifteenth-century German schoolmaster Trebonnius who saw his teaching job as an opportunity to serve. He always treated his students as important people. Each day he began by doffing his hat respectfully to his class. "You students," he said, "are tomorrow's citizens, and who knows what God may do with your lives." One of his students was a boy named Martin Luther.

Even if no Martin Luthers come out of one of Miss Giannetti's classes, her serving spirit glorifies God. Remember, Jesus said, "Whatever you did for one of the least . . . you did for me" (Mt 25:40).

You can also make a difference in jobs that seem far less important than teaching. My daughter Krystal, for instance, once took a job in the school kitchen as a cook/waitress. She decided that with some extra effort on her part, she could make school lunches more tasty. Instead of just thawing and serving french fries—limp and unappetizing—she rotated them in the oven to come out hot and crispy when lunch was served. And instead of letting apple slices wilt on the counter for twenty

38

minutes after preparation, she returned them to the cooler so she could serve them fresh. In short, she gave good service. And children actually came up to her in the kitchen after lunch to thank her.

If you want your work to glorify God, cultivate a spirit of service to others, no matter who they are. If you turn out a product on an assembly line, consider the person who will use that product. It will either serve the user well, or it will disappoint him or her. If it serves well, you will have served well. And Jesus will be pleased.

Glorifying God with Gratitude

You can also glorify God in your work by giving him thanks for it.

My former fishing buddy Glen Thornton has worked for the federal government most of his life—first as a forester, then with the Internal Revenue Service and finally with the Small Business Administration. He's now getting ready to retire.

"How does a Christian in secular work do his work to the glory of God?" I asked Glen recently.

"By giving thanks," Glen replied. "So many workers have such bad attitudes about their jobs. They don't appreciate what they have. They show up at 7:59 to start work at 8:00 and are ready to bolt out the door at 4:29. If you ask them to do anything extra at all, they act like you have stolen their wallet.

"I believe that attitude displeases God," Glen continued. "Being thankful for our jobs glorifies him. We often don't realize how important it is to be grateful to God. Psalm 50:23 says, 'He who sacrifices thank offerings honors me.'

"Of course, I don't like everything about my job. There are always some employees you disagree with or don't like much.

I once had a boss I really disliked, and the feeling was mutual. It rankled him every time I walked past his desk. Yet that boss promoted me three times, and for one simple reason: I kept a good attitude and I did good work.

"I sometimes think of Joseph, whose cruel brothers sold him into slavery in Egypt. He became manager of a high government official's entire household. Then he was unjustly cast into prison but again rose to a position of even higher responsibility— second in command under Pharaoh! At several points Joseph could have justly complained about what a lousy deal he had. He could have worked no more than absolutely necessary. But he didn't. He was trustworthy and dependable, and God honored him."

Glen is right. We glorify God when we demonstrate a spirit of thanksgiving to God for our jobs, even when we have suffered injustice.

Reflecting God's Handiwork

Yet another way we glorify God in our work is by doing a good job.

Recently I have been trying to apply some of the principles I have learned about working to the glory of God around the house. One day I spent several hours working on a lawn mower. I would rather have spent the time writing or working on something that seemed more "spiritual." But I concluded that if the apostle Paul could lay aside some spiritual responsibilities to make tents (see Acts 18:3), I wasn't too important to fix a lawn mower.

I thought I was doing okay on the mower—until I discovered that I'd installed a bearing retainer backward. Because it was rubbing against another part, I knew the mower could not be

40

used that way. To correct the problem I would have to dismantle the machine entirely and start from scratch. I began to get upset.

Then something occurred to me: If I could insert a spacer next to the bearing retainer, the mower would work. I would have to custom-make the spacer, but it would save several hours. In a matter of minutes I had made and installed the spacer, and the mower was working fine.

Suddenly it dawned on me. Even the snag I had encountered helped me glorify God. The Lord had not made an unimaginative robot when he created me. He had made a creative and resourceful problem-solver. I glorified God by using my God-given talents.

The next morning Marge and I negotiated about who would wash the outside of the windows in our second-story bedroom. I quickly lost the argument, being unable to convince even myself that she could place and climb a twenty-foot ladder as well as I could.

"To the glory of God," I reminded myself as I polished those window panes. When I finished I went inside to inspect my work. The tiny dust spatters from earlier rains were gone, along with all the unexplained smudges. The glass gleamed in the sunlight, like a work of art.

The beautiful result of my work made me reflect on God's excellent works. Suddenly I began to see the glory of God all around me. How beautiful that wood grain was on the panels of our doors and cabinets! Like the windows and the lawn mower, our woodwork represented a joint effort of man with God. He made the trees with wood grain wrapped inside, but man milled the wood into panels and then applied a finish that highlighted the grain. When we do good work, we reflect God's excellence.

41

Checking Out Our Own Work

In essence, our work glorifies God whenever we do it

—in obedience to his will

—as a service to others

—with thanks to God for his provision

—in ways that reflect God's creativity and excellence

How does your work stack up against this checklist? If not very well, what will it take to change your situation? You may just need some enlightenment about what God wants of you and a corresponding change of attitude. I hope the enlightenment is in these chapters. The change of attitude is up to you.

For Individuals or Groups

1. The chapter opens with the story of Charles "Buzzy" Morgan who had left the pastorate and was now performing janitorial services. He said that his attitude was the key to "working as unto the Lord," an attitude of obedience. Do you think obedience is the central issue? Explain.

2. Page 32 suggests that even if our work gives us opportunities for witnessing, for supporting God's work financially, or for serving churches or Christian organizations, this is not an adequate way to "work as unto the Lord." Do you agree? Why or why not?

3. Work is not the only kind of obedience God calls us to. Worship is also mentioned (pp. 34-35). As in the case of Mary and Martha, how can we tell when God is calling us to one kind of obedience and not another?

4. How does serving others also glorify God (pp. 36-39)? How could you serve others more in your current job?

5. Why does an attitude of thankfulness also glorify God (pp. 39-40)?

6. How does quality work reflect God's glory—even if no one knows about the extra effort we're putting out?

7. This chapter lists four ways our work can give honor to God. What others can you add?

8. How well do you think your work rates against the checklist on page 42 and the ones you've added? What step can you take this week to begin improvement in one area?

4

When Your Job Involves Moral Compromise

· · · · · · · · ·

*M*ost jobs—*whether humble or prestigious, blue-collar* or white-collar—demand some kind of moral compromise. This means you'll be making hard choices if you are trying to glorify God in your work.

Before we examine the different ways you can approach an unethical work situation, let's consider some real-life stories of Christian employees who got caught in compromising positions.

Case of the Corporate Shenanigans
Arnold was chief financial officer of a company with seventeen hundred employees and $400 million in annual sales. After a couple of years on the job, he began discovering practices that

disturbed him. For one thing, the company was mismanaging the employee retirement fund in a way that put employees at risk with the Internal Revenue Service. For another, the company was using incorrect and unfair accounting procedures. Arnold also discovered that certain customers were receiving preferential treatment.

Arnold felt responsible and wanted to correct these inequities. Although acknowledging he was right, others in top management continually dragged their feet. Then Arnold discovered actual misappropriation of company resources by one executive. He demanded action and got it, but still sensed he was working against continued resistance.

Arnold became more and more convinced that those in control lacked integrity. His own role had become a negative one; he was always raising troublesome questions that no one else seemed concerned about.

Arnold stayed in his post for eleven years. During that time he influenced company policy to the benefit of employees and stockholders. Both groups would have otherwise suffered from the actions of executives who were only looking out for themselves.

Still, the constant tension and conflict wore on him. Arnold did not relish his watchdog role, and often felt hypocritical for being part of an unprincipled management team. Business conflicts absorbed him to the point that his marriage, family and church life suffered.

Arnold considered quitting for a long time. He was one of the highest paid financial executives in his field, and he knew that if he left his job, he would probably have to take a pay cut. Over fifty and overqualified, he might have difficulty finding any position.

Finally Arnold decided he had to resign. At this writing, some fifteen months later, he still has not found a permanent position.

Case of the Not-So-Solid Brick Wall

John Younglove is a bricklayer who has always prided himself on the quality of his work. When competition in the building trades became especially keen, John's boss began putting him under more pressure to produce. The only way John could meet those demands for speed was to cut corners—to mortar the bricks in such a way that, though the job looked good initially, it would not stand up well over the years.

The other workers seemed willing to go along with the boss's demands. John knew that he would have to produce or lose his job. He agonized over what to do. Working for another builder wouldn't help; they were all cutting corners to stay competitive. He decided to increase his productivity while maintaining his quality standards. This caused him to work under extreme stress, and he still came in at the low end of acceptable output.

John wondered whether he should compromise his standards in order to keep working at his trade. As wrong as that seemed, it was better than letting his family go on welfare, wasn't it? Only one other option came to mind: he could start his own business. He was scared to take the risk, but after much prayer and consultation with others, he decided to become an independent contractor.

He has never been sorry. After twelve years, he is still as busy laying bricks—the right way—as he wants to be.

Case of the Blasphemous Book

Librarian Veronica Lewis believes in intellectual freedom. In

45

fact, she often catalogs books with which she strongly disagrees. One book on witchcraft, however, she found not only to be blasphemous but without redeeming value. As she thought about her role in making that book available, Veronica was troubled by Jesus' words: "Woe to the world because of the things that cause people to sin! Such things must come, but woe to the man through whom they come!" (Mt 18:7). She certainly did not want to help promote witchcraft in any way that might cause someone to turn away from God.

Ultimately, Veronica decided that agreeing to catalog a few objectionable books did not mean she approved of them. Although she could not control the content of every book in the library, she enjoyed helping people find the many worthwhile books the library offered and stuck with her job.

Case of the Twisted Story

Marla is an editor. The publisher she works for decided to put out a book in support of a cause she considers questionable. Marla was assigned the task of editing the book—of making it as polished and persuasive as she could. She began the work, but in the process became even more skeptical about it. She believed that the author was distorting facts to make his case seem stronger than it really was.

Marla accepted the principle that the books she edited did not have to fully reflect her personal convictions. After all, they were published in the name of the author and represented the author's views, not the editor's. But helping to publish false information was quite different from simply helping someone present a view she did not share.

After expressing her opposition to the book several times, Marla was told that the decision was firm; the book would be published. Feeling secure in her job and strong in her convictions, Marla finally asked her boss to assign the book to another editor. Her boss honored her request, and their work relationship remained intact.

Case of the Misleading Sales Pitch

Janet was a telemarketer. She believed in the product she was selling, but not in the sales pitch her boss taught her to use. She knew it was less than one hundred per cent truthful. Her trainer said that stretching the truth a bit didn't matter because the pitch only worked with people who really wanted to buy; she was just giving them the little extra reason they needed to do it now instead of later.

At first Janet tried not to be bothered by her misleading sales pitch. As she grew in her Christian life, however, she became concerned about it. When the women's fellowship at her church asked Janet to consider becoming an officer, it precipitated a personal crisis for her. She didn't feel she could accept such a position while living in disobedience to God. But she also doubted she could sell her product without "exaggerating."

Janet tried using total truthfulness in her presentation. When she had used the prescribed sales pitch, she was one of the better producers in the company. Without it, her success rate dropped drastically.

Janet finally decided to quit her job. "Ninety-five per cent of my sales pitch is true," she told me, "but it's the other five per cent that closes the sales."

Analyzing Our Cases

The above cases suggest several ways a person can deal with unethical job situations. At least four possibilities exist:

47

1. *Sell out.* Do what the job requires and don't allow ethical questions to interfere with your work. Janet, the telephone solicitor, did this for a while until her conscience prompted her to take a stand. John, the bricklayer, considered selling out when he couldn't think of any good alternative.

2. *Compromise.* Do what you can to be a good influence, even though you have to put up with some things that you feel are wrong to keep your job. Arnold, the corporate executive, did this for about nine years, and in retrospect he believes he accomplished a lot of good. Veronica, the librarian, decided that making worthwhile books available to people outweighed the evil of cataloging a few offensive books.

3. *Negotiate.* Work within an imperfect system, but enter into dialog with supervisors when necessary to avoid personal involvement in wrongdoing. Marla, the editor, asked her boss to get someone else to edit the book she believed to be dishonest. Negotiating enabled her to stick to her principles without quitting.

4. *Quit.* The bricklayer, the telemarketer and the corporate treasurer ultimately quit their jobs rather than participate in enterprises they considered unethical.

Let's discuss each of these four options in more detail.

Selling Out

Since selling out disobeys God, we need not even discuss it, right?

Wrong. We can't dismiss selling out so easily. Christians sometimes sell out just as others do.

Of course, most of us never actually say, "I will sell out my principles for the sake of my job." Instead, we rationalize. We gloss over what's really happening. We think of ourselves as basically decent people whose good intentions make up for whatever wrongdoing our job demands. We believe integrity is wonderful—just awfully inconvenient on the job.

When Bill Petersen wrote the first installment of a career column in *Eternity* magazine entitled "Nine to Five," he told of leading an adult Sunday-school discussion some years before:

I asked what problems the members of my adult class had as they tried to apply Christian principles to their jobs.

I was surprised—maybe appalled is a better word—by lack of response.

Certainly someone in the group of 25 must be facing some job-related challenges. I started probing deeper. I asked a salesman about some questionable practices in his field. He responded frankly that those things didn't bother him. His job was to sell. Whatever it took to make the sale was OK with him. He had been a faithful church member and professing Christian for years, but had never let his Christianity intrude upon the hours of 9 to 5.

I take that back. He may have occasionally spoken a word for Jesus Christ or passed out a gospel tract. But as far as allowing Scripture to examine his business conduct, that was not in his mind.[1]

"Not in his mind." Selling out bothers us less when we manage to keep it out of our minds. Like the salesman in Bill Petersen's class, the telemarketer in our earlier story didn't give her situation much thought until God got her attention and made her face the issue.

Have you considered whether your work situation involves you in wrongdoing? If not, are you afraid of what you might see if you examined your job too closely?

You can also sell out by examining your job but deceiving

yourself about what you see. Have you ever wondered why only the doctors employed by tobacco companies doubt whether smoking causes heart and lung disease? Or why executives of nuclear, chemical and industrial plants typically see less danger to their neighbors or the environment than outside observers do? These employees may not be lying. Rather, their self-interest may have colored their thinking and predisposed them to faulty conclusions. They may have half-consciously or unconsciously "sold out."

You may not only need to examine your job, but to recognize that you may be incapable of impartial judgment. Perhaps you need to give more weight to the evaluations of Christian peers than to your own. Ask some caring brothers and sisters in Christ to help you work through the issues involved.

Pure as the Driven Snow

At the opposite pole from those who refuse to face the moral issues involved in their jobs are those who say, "I will have nothing whatsoever to do with moral compromise in any form. And neither should any other Christian."

That may seem a totally admirable position to take. Still, I wonder: Does this stance represent true moral integrity or naive self-righteousness?

I believe Scripture gives us direction through this moral minefield. In other words, we can be principled people (even if not totally "untainted") and still function in the world as it is.

Remember Paul's admonitions to believers to stay in the workplace, which we discussed in chapter two. Paul told the Thessalonians they should work with their hands and not be idle. Anticipation of the Lord's soon return was not a valid reason to exchange a job-holding lifestyle for a "these-are-the-last-days" concentration on spiritual things.

Paul's later instruction to the Corinthians was similar but given in a context more to the point here. The question at Corinth was not so much, How should we live in light of the Lord's soon return? It was rather, How should we live in light of our conversion? Since old things have passed away for us, can we still participate in this world's system? Can we continue living with unsaved mates, working for unbelieving masters, and functioning in an ungodly culture?

As you may recall, Paul answered that new Christians do not necessarily need to change their life circumstances. "Each one should retain the place in life that the Lord assigned to him and to which God has called him. This is the rule I lay down in all the churches" (1 Cor 7:17).

Paul specifically applies this *Corinthian concept,* as we might call it, to one's marital state, to one's circumcision (or lack thereof), and to one's condition of servitude, which most closely resembles a job situation in our own day. Scripture does teach, then, that though most jobs in our fallen world involve some degree of complicity with evil, we as Christians should not withdraw from the workplace. We need to learn when to compromise, when to negotiate and when to quit a particular job.

Think of the most inoffensive of occupations, and you will probably find it involves some complicity with evil if you look hard enough. Mailmen often deliver pornographic magazines, advertisements for products of dubious value, and anything else not specifically prohibited by postal regulations. Supermarket clerks enable people to purchase cigarettes, junk food, trashy tabloids and other harmful items. And as we saw, even librarians help people find and use books that espouse ungodly views.

Realistically, ethical dilemmas on the job leave us with the three viable options we have already mentioned. We can find an acceptable compromise (like Veronica the librarian), negotiate our way out of direct involvement with wrongdoing (like Marla the editor), or we can quit the job in favor of another job we hope will prove better (like John the bricklayer).

Actually, compromising and negotiating both involve some degree of compromise. For example, though Marla refused to edit the objectionable book, she compromised to a degree by continuing to work for the same company at all. As an employee, she has a degree of complicity in everything her employer publishes. Still, doing evil and being associated with those who do evil are not synonymous. We must not do the first, but we can hardly avoid the second.

Daniel's Dilemma

There is biblical precedent for compromising and negotiating on the job, as we can see in the case of Daniel, who avoided active participation in wrongdoing even though he worked in the less-than-righteous pagan government of Babylon. Daniel was one of several Hebrew young men selected "to be trained for three years, and after that they were to enter the king's service" (Dan 1:5).

A problem arose when the royal diet prescribed for Daniel included food he considered unclean. "Daniel resolved not to defile himself with the royal food and wine" (v.8). Though he had made up his mind not to eat the king's food, Daniel did not simply defy the establishment. He did not take a belligerent or hostile approach, attacking the system as Satanic. Nor did he play the self-righteous hero and announce, "I am not going to eat this stuff no matter what you do; I'm obeying God."

Instead Daniel "asked the chief official for permission not to defile himself this way" (v. 8). The official's response was not as positive as Daniel had hoped. The chief official liked him (Daniel's attitude probably had a lot to do with that), but didn't dare alter the king's policy. It could cost him his head if the king saw Daniel looking worse than the other young men.

This response undoubtedly discouraged Daniel, but he didn't give up. He found in the official's words a clue that he could use. The official's real concern was about the *effects* of Daniel's diet—not the specific foods he ate. The king only cared that Daniel stay robust.

Conflict resolution often hinges on detecting the real desires of the involved parties as distinguished from the immediate issues dividing them. Finding a way to meet these underlying desires opens the way to resolving the issues at conflict.

Daniel believed that he and his companions could be as healthy on their diet of kosher foods as on the king's menu. To demonstrate this, he proposed a ten-day test. "Give us nothing but vegetables to eat and water to drink. Then compare our appearance with that of the young men who eat the royal food, and treat your servants in accordance with what you see" (vv. 12-13).

Daniel did not make this proposal to the same chief official who had denied his earlier request. He went down the chain of command to his immediate supervisor. You have heard of going over the head of your boss? That may be necessary sometimes, but it usually alienates your boss. Daniel did the opposite. He went to the guard was directly responsible for implementing policy—who actually knew and controlled what Daniel would eat and drink.

Scripture doesn't tell us why Daniel did this, and it may seem sneaky on his part. However, Daniel could have been acting out of consideration for the chief official, who had expressed concern for his head if he granted Daniel's request. This way the chief official was in the clear. He had not deviated from the king's command. He didn't even know about Daniel's deal with the guard.

In any event, everything turned out happily. At the end of the ten-day test, Daniel "looked healthier and better nourished" than those on the king's diet.

If it had come right down to hard choices, Daniel would have refused, I believe, to eat the king's food. But with patience, resourcefulness and a positive attitude, he worked out a resolution satisfactory to all concerned. God later used Daniel greatly in a high government position, something he would not likely have attained had he simply refused to cooperate with the authorities.

Is there some way you also might resolve the moral conflict in your job? Pray for wisdom to see what your employer's real aims are and how you can help achieve them without compromising your standards. Do not approach your superiors with hostility, accusations or self-righteous anger. And do not hastily quit your job. Walking out might close doors that compromise and negotiation would keep open for future ministry and witness.

Daniel has gone down in history as a man of great integrity. On one occasion he refused to stop praying to God even when the penalty was to be cast into a den of hungry lions. But Daniel also negotiated with and participated in a pagan system. "Daring to be a Daniel" will require that you resolutely stick to your principles. It will also require that you show the courage to negotiate and work with people whose actions you may heartily disapprove.

A Good Job of Quitting

In our early examples, three people ultimately quit their jobs—the bricklayer, the telephone solicitor, and the corporation treasurer. All came to the place where they felt they could not change matters enough to make the job acceptable.

Perhaps they could have come up with an acceptable compromise had they been as resourceful as Daniel. Maybe not. Sometimes quitting is the best or only option. Still, we can do a good or bad job of quitting.

If you decide to quit, make sure you've taken enough time to work through your decision. Though some wrongs may be so blatant that you feel compelled to quit on the spot, most situations will allow you to weigh the issues, think of the consequences and make tentative plans for the future. Be sure to get counsel from family, respected friends and (where appropriate) trusted coworkers.

You should count the cost before quitting. God may reward you for your integrity by providing you another, better job. But, as in Arnold's case, he might not. You cannot manipulate God to reward you directly for doing the right thing. Can you accept that without growing bitter and angry?

If you do decide to quit, leave as congenially as possible. Give appropriate notice and continue working faithfully to the end. You may need a good reference from this employer someday, if not immediately. You may even want to return to this same company eventually.

Avoid judging those you are leaving behind as evil people or weak compromisers. Simply express your own convictions: "I feel I cannot in good conscience do this or that, or support such and such a policy." This way you make your principles known without presuming to tell others what they should or should not do.

Tough Choices

Ethical dilemmas in the workplace rarely lend themselves to black-and-white answers. It might be easier if God had given us hard and fast guidance to avoid or quit any job that hinted at moral compromise. But he tells us to stay in our present jobs unless the degree of evil we must live with compels us to leave. By forcing us to decide whether we should compromise, negotiate or quit in a given situation, God refines our discernment and causes us to lean on him as we ask for wisdom.

God will guide you step by step as you submit to him. As you pass through the wilderness of tough choices, remember Proverbs 3:5-6: "Trust in the Lord with all your heart and lean not on your own understanding; in all your ways acknowledge him, and he will make your paths straight."

In all your ways, acknowledge him—by asking for his direction, by committing yourself to his will, by making him Lord of your work situation. And he will make your paths straight.

For Individuals or Groups

1. When have you been faced with a situation involving ethical compromise at work? If you resolved the problem, how did you do so? If not, why not?

2. As you look at the case studies at the beginning of the chapter, which people, if any, do you think made wrong decisions? Explain.

3. The first option mentioned for dealing with ethical dilemmas is selling out (pp. 48-50). Do you think the tendency to sell out (without a guilty conscience) can affect Christians as much as anyone? Why or why not?

4. Think again about your job. The black-and-white moral questions are easy to spot. What are some of the gray areas where you work?

5. On page 51 the author says, "Think of the most inoffensive of occupations, and you will probably find it involves some complicity with evil if you look hard enough." Do you agree that no job is completely untainted? Explain.

6. How did Daniel compromise and negotiate his way out of a dilemma (pp. 52-54)? What principles from Daniel's experience do you find helpful and why?

7. If you do decide to quit, what should you keep in mind (p. 55)? What else would you say is important to do before you quit?

8. What action, if any, will you take regarding an ethical issue you face on the job?

5

Getting Along with Your Boss

· · · · · · · ·

A *lmost everybody who works has a boss. Even the pres-*
ident of a company usually reports to a board of directors.

Your relationship with your boss can tremendously affect your
attitude toward your job. If you are going to enjoy your work—
and consciously glorify God in it by being a good employee—
you must learn how to relate to your boss. Let's consider the
whole issue of boss/employee relations more fully.

A Success Story

In the early 1970s I became a boss. As a middle-management
editor at Scripture Press, I supervised several editorial workers.
One was a young former sportswriter named Jerry Jenkins.

Jerry, a capable and quick-witted worker, got off to a somewhat rocky start. His constant wisecracks, even in planning meetings, bothered one of the senior editors. Then I overheard him talking at length on the telephone in what was clearly a personal call on company time. I shot him a memo taking him to task on it.

Jerry responded immediately. "Though I did not initiate the call, I realize I talked too long," he told me. "It won't happen again, and I'll be staying after work tonight to make up the time."

Later I grew concerned about the quality of Jerry's work. I hardly ever found fault with his editing; the changes he made were consistently appropriate. But he didn't go far enough. He polished the writing a little, but didn't seem to have his heart set on making each story or article the strongest piece he could. I found myself making extensive editorial suggestions.

I didn't mind at first; after all, he was learning. After a few months, however, I received a manuscript which he had edited even more lightly than usual. I sent it back with some suggestions for changes and asked to see it again before publication. When he returned it to me, I was upset. Jerry had only minimally implemented my suggestions. I decided to edit the piece myself.

After I had given a copy of the re-edited piece to Jerry, he came to see me. "I don't understand," he said. "You made more changes in this story the second time through than both of us did together the first time."

"The story had a lot more potential than you were getting out of it," I explained. "It needed to be reorganized, not just copyedited. I want you to make these pieces the best you can before you send them on to me. I don't want you depending on me to catch a lot of things."

Jerry got the message, and the quality of his work improved markedly.

Since then, Jerry Jenkins has risen rapidly in the field of Christian publishing. Today he is not only a widely published author, but vice president of Moody Bible Institute, responsible for the publishing division which includes *Moody Monthly* magazine, Moody bookstores and Moody Press.

I think Jerry's success came in part because he had a great attitude toward his boss, and a very Christian attitude, I might add. Based partly on his example, then, here are some guidelines for dealing with your boss.

Respond Positively When Corrected

We read in Proverbs, "A rebuke impresses a man of discernment more than a hundred lashes a fool" (17:10). Discerning workers think twice about how they react to their boss's criticism; he or she may possibly have a point. Anyhow, as the old saying puts it, "The boss may not always be right, but he is always the boss." If we want to get along with the boss, we must consider what he has to say.

Remember Jerry's reaction to being corrected? In the telephone episode, he could have responded defensively to my memo. He could have complained that if I hadn't eavesdropped, I would not have known about his conversation in the first place. Or he could have been overcome with guilt and self-reproach. He could have thought, "Oh, great, I'm in trouble with my boss already. He doesn't like me! I've blown my chances of succeeding in this job."

Instead, Jerry faced the issue squarely, neither minimizing nor exaggerating his offense. And he promptly took action to do what he could to make up for his error. I respected him for

61

volunteering to make up the time he had spent talking on the telephone.

Jerry also responded positively when I re-edited his manuscript. He didn't just shrug off my puzzling behavior. He came and asked questions until he understood the reasons for my actions.

Your boss will probably correct you at times. When he or she does, you can take that potentially painful and unpleasant experience and turn it to your advantage by responding positively. If the criticism is valid, you can turn it into a double advantage. First, you can take it to heart and improve your performance. Second, you can win your boss's respect by keeping a humble attitude.

If your boss's criticism does not ring true, you face a tougher situation; we'll explore how to deal with unfair treatment in the next chapter of this book. Even when your boss treats you unfairly, however, you can still make the best of a bad situation by keeping your own attitude right. This brings us to the next point.

Cultivate a Positive Attitude

When Jerry and I worked together at Scripture Press, Lloyd Cory was editorial vice president. Lloyd was the "big boss" about three levels above Jerry. None of us knew it at the time, but Lloyd told me later about one of the little things that set Jerry apart favorably in his mind.

Lloyd usually arrived early for work at his office overlooking the editorial employees' parking lot. That meant Lloyd could see us as we walked from our cars into the building. "I noticed Jerry always coming to work with a smile on his face," Lloyd said. "And I thought, there's something special about that guy. You can tell he enjoys working here." When Lloyd was looking for someone to promote into management, he remembered Jerry's attitude toward his job.

Jerry also kept a positive attitude toward me. "You know how a boss can make an employee look good to the rest of the company, sometimes even cover for his mistakes?" he remarked to me once. "I believe an employee can make his boss look good too, and that's what I want to do."

As I thought about it, I realized he was right. A boss whose workers produce well, make few mistakes and have good attitudes will probably look very good in the eyes of his supervisors.

If you want to get along famously with your boss, try to make him or her look good. Your boss will probably love you for it. (At some point you may want to tell your boss about your desire to make him look good, just as Jerry did. Some of us bosses are a little slow to notice things like that.)

Step into Your Boss's Shoes

By trying to make his boss look good, Jerry was applying the Golden Rule to the workplace. Jesus said, "Do to others as you would have them do to you" (Lk 6:31). Treating your boss as you would want to be treated if you were the boss will help build a solid relationship.

If you were a boss, would you want your workers to make you look bad to your superiors? Talk about you disparagingly to other workers? Resist direction in a peevish or hostile manner? Butter you up or manipulate you for their own purposes? Try to undermine your authority? Scheme to get rid of you?

Since you would not want to be treated in these ways, you cannot in good conscience turn around and treat your boss in these ways.

Stepping into your employer's shoes means making his concerns your own. Typically, employers are concerned about the bottom line. Talk all you want about fair wages and good benefits; if an employer is losing money, he will soon be out of business and many others will be out of jobs. U.S. industrial workers, for example, negotiated favorable work contracts with steel makers only to find their industry becoming less and less competitive with foreign steel. The result: their plants closed and they lost their jobs.

Whether you work for big business or the corner store, you have to help make your employer a profit if he is going to keep you on the job. Once again, we come back to the Golden Rule. If you owned a company, wouldn't you want your workers to take an interest in making the company profitable?

My wife Marge works for a gift shop called Made In Oregon, which sells items exclusively made, grown or caught in Oregon. Marge could, of course, simply do the minimum required of her—wait on customers and let it go at that. Instead she constantly keeps the best interests of her employer in mind. She takes initiative to mark down and sell damaged merchandise instead of discarding it or giving it away. She gives out free samples judiciously. And she suggests purchases to customers, who often buy more as a result.

Marge does not have to do these things. She does not work on a commission, and no one even keeps track of her personal sales. But to her, working for a company means serving that company's best interests. She treats management the way she would like to be treated if she were management.

It's amazing how up-to-date and far-ranging the Golden Rule is—until you remember it was Jesus' idea. I think he was on to something.

Bridge the Boss Gap

Someone might ask whether Jesus' words really apply to employee/boss relationships. After all, doesn't everyone recognize that the work force is divided into two classes: labor and management? And aren't these two antagonists?

The designations of labor and management do divide people. As Christians, however, we need to see the situation from God's perspective.

Various distinctions besides labor and management separate people from one another: male and female, young and old, Jews and Gentiles, conservatives and liberals, rich and poor, blacks and whites, and on and on. By nature we tend to discriminate against (and even dehumanize) people who are not like us. When this happens, we may live according to the Golden Rule in our relationships with peers while not even seeing others (bosses, for example) as people.

The gospel cuts across all these boundaries: "There is neither Jew nor Greek, slave nor free, male nor female, for you are all one in Christ Jesus" (Gal 3:28). Obviously distinctions remain between these people groups that Scripture says "are all one." Paul is not saying that these distinctions should not exist, but that we as Christians should be breaking down the barriers that divide people. As Paul wrote elsewhere, "For [Jesus] is our peace, who has made the two one and has destroyed the barrier, the dividing wall of hostility" (Eph 2:14).

There it is! The barrier. The dividing wall. The hostility. That is what Christ removes. In Christ we can no longer view others as wholly separate from us, but as human beings with feelings, loved by God and entitled to be treated with respect.

Is that how you see your boss?

As a Christian, your respectful attitude toward superiors can help break down labor/management barriers, while still acknowledging the distinctions. This is part of what it means to recognize Christ as Lord of the workplace.

When All Else Fails

If you respond positively when corrected, cultivate a good attitude, treat your boss like you would want to be treated, and try to break down barriers between labor and management, what boss won't like you?

Unfortunately, there are some.

What should you do when, because of personality conflicts or other reasons, your best efforts do not produce a happy relationship between you and your boss? In that case, the following admonition from Scripture seems appropriate: "Slaves, submit yourselves to your masters with all respect, not only to those who are good and considerate, but also to those who are harsh. For it is commendable if a man bears up under the pain of unjust suffering because he is conscious of God" (1 Pet 2:18-19).

You, of course, are not a slave, and you shouldn't just roll over and put up with abuse. What we learn from this passage, rather, is that Christians should demonstrate respect for those in authority, no matter what kind of people they are. Your difficult boss may drive you to quit, but as long as you work for him, treat him with respect. It's not a question of what kind of person he is. It's a question of what kind of person *you* are—someone who "is conscious of God."

A Third Party is involved in your relationship with your boss. Both of you will ultimately answer to him. So respect your boss, regardless of his or her behavior, remembering you will answer to God only for yourself.

For Individuals or Groups

1. Who was your worst boss and why? How did you cope with the situation?

2. The author says Jerry Jenkins had a great attitude toward his boss (pp. 59-63). What made that attitude so good?

3. How would you rate your attitude toward your current boss? What one step could you take this week to improve it?

4. If you traded places with your boss, what would you want from your employee?

5. On page 65 we read, "Obviously distinctions remain between these people groups [Jew and Greek, slave and free, male and female] that Scripture says 'are all one.' " What are some of the differences between bosses and those who work under them? How can these differences be bridged?

6. What are some alternatives to quitting if you and your boss hit an impasse over some issue?

7. How can you judge when it is time to quit because of a problem with your boss?

6
Overcoming Unfair Treatment

· · · · · · · ·

*F*aye *works as a clerk in a retail store chain that was* recently considering unionization. During that time of uncertainty, the big boss often mingled with the workers. He even wrote Faye and the other employees glowing letters in which he described the "family atmosphere" he hoped to create in the store. He also encouraged them to come to him personally if they had any problems or questions. In the end, his efforts helped persuade the employees not to unionize.

Shortly after that decision was made, Faye approached her manager about receiving her modest annual raise. The manager contacted her supervisor at company headquarters, who said, yes, Faye would get her raise.

The next payday, no raise appeared. Faye asked why. The manager didn't know, but she promised to remind the supervisor.

The next payday, again no raise. Faye asked why and got the same answer as before. That run-around continued for two months. Finally the manager told Faye to go to the supervisor herself.

Good luck trying! Faye couldn't get through on the telephone, and when she left a message her calls were not returned. She later learned that other employees had tried to reach the supervisor or the big boss himself and gotten nowhere. In reality, neither of them cared much about the store clerks.

When the top management says one thing and does another, low-ranking workers, as well as middle managers, lose. A Christian manager who wants to treat employees right may be frustrated by policies and practices implemented at higher levels.

A Question of Respect

Workers like Faye often complain that supervisors do not treat them with respect. But breaking faith is only one way managers show lack of respect for employees. Verbal abuse is another.

Recently I visited an auto wrecking yard to get a better seat for my 1963 Corvair van. Since I had to remove the seat from a wrecked vehicle, I was on the premises a while—long enough to hear the boss chew out several employees.

One worker didn't come quickly enough when the boss yelled for him. The boss reprimanded another for selling an item too cheaply. Then he accused a third of goofing off because he took too long to remove a part.

I witnessed half a dozen exchanges between that employer and his workers; every comment he made was belittling. As I was leaving, I heard the boss make a threat: "Somebody won't be working here any more after today."

Who would want to work here? I thought. I didn't even want to trade there again, much less put up with that man's abuse every day.

Lack of respect for employees can also surface in a condescending attitude. Caryl Silverthorne works as a nurse at a major urban medical center. Morale has dropped there, and management says they're concerned about it. But what do they do? Treat employees as intelligent people who might have something worthwhile to say by giving them an opportunity to be heard?

No. They simply announce they will recognize staff members' birthdays by providing a cake. "All that involves," says Caryl, "is sending a note to the dietician to get so-and-so a cake. Big deal. And so far, they haven't even followed through on that."

Employers most commonly show lack of respect for their workers by paying them too little. We once assumed that only the unemployed were poor. With the increased cost of maintaining a home and the decrease in high-paying jobs, however, the 1980s saw the emergence of a working poor class and even a working homeless class in the United States. More and more full-time workers could not afford the cost of a home.

Paul writes that each person "must work, doing something useful with his own hands, that he may have something to share with those in need" (Eph 4:28). But work does not always provide the worker with "something to share." The homeless and working poor do not make enough to live decently, let alone to share with others. In those cases, work is not serving all the purposes God intends.

As Christians, we can at least raise awareness about the plight of underpaid workers and support efforts to help them. Minimum wage laws, while not necessarily the best answer, are one mechanism by which society can seek to provide workers with a livable return from their labor.

Finally, women experience more than their share of disrespect. Employers have traditionally paid them less and given them fewer responsibilities than their male counterparts. If a woman does rise to management, her attempts to be firm or forthright with male employees may bruise their fragile egos and make them defensive.

Unfortunately, a woman often must work harder than a man to establish respect. Tests indicate, for example, that subordinates view hostility and dominance as more acceptable in male leaders than in female leaders. In one woman's office, I saw a sign which reads, "A woman has to produce twice as much as a man to get the same benefits. Fortunately, that's not difficult." A bit of reverse sexism, there, but some truth too.

Dealing adequately with the special problems of women in the workplace goes beyond the scope of this book, as well as beyond the capabilities of this author. (Never having been a woman in the workplace, I can't fully appreciate what it's like.) A book that I think addresses the subject well is *But Can She Type?* by Janet L. Kobobel (InterVarsity Press). This book, subtitled "Overcoming Stereotypes in the Workplace," focuses on women who are in (or moving toward) management roles. One chapter, entitled "Women Wielding Power," deals with the difficulty women sometimes face working with male peers or subordinates.

Disrespect for employees—in the form of dishonesty, abuse, condescension, underpayment or discrimination—is, at bottom, a spiritual problem. Obviously, Christian managers should take extra care to demonstrate respect for their employees. The Bible teaches that God made every person in his image and gave each worth and dignity. Paul emphasized that even slaves should be treated with respect: "Masters, provide your slaves with what is right and fair, because you know that you also have a Master in heaven" (Col 4:1; see also Eph 6:9).

Employers should play fair not only because it is right, but because it serves their organization's best interests. I wouldn't want workers who feel I am defrauding or otherwise misusing them to handle my money or goods. Says Faye, the clerk who didn't get her promised raise: "Believe me, if I weren't honest, I could steal so much stuff. And when they treat me unfairly, I think about it. Other employees do steal; I'm sure of it. Management is so shortsighted!"

Wrong Solutions

John needed a job but was having trouble finding one that paid enough. He had worked before in the produce department of a grocery store but had quit because the pay was so low. Desperate, he decided to reapply for such a position, even though he still resented the low wages.

Finally he found an opening. "I'll pay you $140 a week to manage my produce section," the grocer said.

John was ready. "Okay, I'll take $140."

And that's just what he did. "The grocer paid $140, and I took $140," John recalls. "That gave me $280 a week, which was just about a livable wage."

Workers commonly respond to unfair treatment by ripping off the company. Scripture, on the other hand, teaches that the Christian "must steal no longer" but support himself by honest and productive work (Eph 4:28).

Christians who would not steal under ordinary circumstances

73

sometimes feel justified in "evening things up" with their employers. In essence, they exalt themselves to the position of judge in their own case against the company. In a court of law, a judge who has a personal stake in a case must disqualify himself because his views may be colored by self-interest. When people cheat or steal on the job and imagine they are justified, they unfairly pronounce a verdict in their own favor ("I should be paid more") and decree that their employer's property be confiscated to satisfy that judgment.

Employees respond to unfair treatment in various other undesirable ways besides stealing. One way to get even with an unfair employer is to retaliate with poor performance: "If they won't pay me what my work is worth, I'll make my work worth what they pay me."

Reducing the volume or quality of your work, however, smacks of vengeance, which the Bible forbids (see Rom 12:19). And dragging your feet on the job also violates the basic biblical principle for work which we discussed at length in chapter one: "Whatever you do, work at it with all your heart, as working for the Lord, not for men" (Col 3:23).

A Plan of Action

How should you respond to unfair treatment on the job? Here are some suggestions to help you get perspective about your situation. (These suggestions are not necessarily listed in the order you should implement them. Actually, you will probably want to pursue several of them at the same time.)

Pray. God is sovereign and can work on your behalf. Scripture teaches, "In everything, by prayer and petition, with thanksgiving, present your requests to God" (Phil 4:6).

Pray first and foremost for grace to handle the situation in a manner worthy of a child of God. Pray that you won't give in to the temptation to steal or hate or retaliate. Pray for wisdom to know what to do, step by step, in seeking resolution of your problem. And pray that God will bring glory to himself through the situation.

Talk with a confidant. God is your most trusted confidant. However, you can also find help by talking with other people.

Think twice about whom you choose as a confidant rather than badmouthing the company to anyone who will listen. You can get different kinds of help from different people. For example, a spouse who listens to your work-related woes and gives you moral support may be your day-to-day confidant. But a spouse who does not understand the work you do probably can't give valid feedback concerning a dispute about your job performance. In that case, you're more likely to find a wise confidant among coworkers or friends in a professional or trade organization.

When you confide in someone, don't just complain. Instead, say something like this: "I have a problem at work, and I need to talk it over with you. I don't want or expect you to solve the problem for me; just listen and see if what I say makes any sense. Maybe I'm the one whose thinking is wrong."

The question you need answered is this: Is my place of employment characterized by an unhealthy, exploitative climate— or is it a pretty good place to work despite the fact that I am feeling misused right now? You don't want to paint your whole job situation black if you are only focusing on one black smudge.

Whether any solutions come from such a conversation or not, you will probably feel better after talking through your frustrations. For a more detailed treatment of how helpful it can be to confide in other people, you might want to read the book *Burn-out* by Ayala M. Pines and Elliot Aronson with Ditsa Kafry (Mac-Millan, 1981).

Go to your boss about it. Don't assume that your boss knows what's troubling you. Even if you have already told him, don't assume he understands how important the issue is to you. If possible, talk things out. Don't just state the facts as you see them, but also explain how you feel.

Unfortunately, some bosses aren't easy to talk to, especially if festering problems have seriously damaged the relationship already. Go to your boss early rather than waiting until the problem becomes unbearable.

Use established grievance procedures. Some companies lay out established procedures for resolving employee grievances. If your employer provides such a system, use it first.

If no internal remedies are available (or if grievance procedures are, in practice, ineffective) look to outside agencies. Most jurisdictions in the United States have fair labor laws to protect workers. If you have been misused, the state labor department may go to bat for you. For example, employers cannot withhold earned wages except under strictly controlled conditions. It is also against the law for an employer to discriminate against you because of your sex, race or religion.

Keep appropriate records. If you have an on-the-job grievance, keep records about it. Instead of just speaking with your boss, write him a memo detailing your case. After any relevant meeting, write a memo giving an account of decisions made or policies expressed; then send it to your boss and a copy to anyone else directly involved. Keep a copy of it for your own file as well, and indicate that you are doing so on the memo itself. (Just type "cc:file" at the bottom.)

Your "paper trail" need not indicate a hostile or confrontational spirit. It is simply good procedure. You obviously need to use discretion; putting words in writing gives them more power and permanence. Don't be abusive of others or harsh in your charges or complaints. And don't create something that can easily be used against you. Keeping written records should only attest to what has transpired and demonstrate the good spirit in which you have acted.

Remember Faye, the store clerk who got the run-around about her annual raise? She eventually wrote a letter to the supervisor factually outlining her complaint in a conciliatory tone. Shortly after that, the supervisor called her manager, praised the spirit of Faye's letter and authorized her raise retroactive to the date when it was first promised.

Know when it's time to move on. Not all job conflicts can be resolved. When they can't, the worker must decide whether he should leave.

The workplace, like the world, is never completely fair. We have to live with imperfection and various inequities. We do not, however, have to live with continual abuse.

Sue, a leader in a Christian organization, was dedicated, bright and efficient. The president began to consider her for an important post that involved a promotion.

The president told Sue about his plans for her, and she understood that he was offering her the new post. The president, however, had not made a final decision. Over the next weeks, he thought he detected an ambitious spirit in her that offended him.

Eventually he denied Sue the promotion on the grounds that she did not have a servant spirit. In fact, he told her he feared she was power hungry. Sue was more grieved over the reason

77

for her rejection than over the decision itself. She had completely committed herself to the concept of servant leadership.

"We have a communication problem," she told the president. "I am sure you have misunderstood me. But if you are right, if I am power hungry in ways I do not see, please point out to me what I have done that reveals this about me."

The president would not respond. He would not help her see where she had been wrong, if, indeed, she had been. Because of his silence, Sue decided she could neither respect nor accept his decision. She saw no other recourse but to resign. As hurt as she was, she purposed not to gossip about the president or the organization. That, she knew, would be wrong.

You too may have to quit a job—or even face getting fired— under unjust circumstances. If so, remember Joseph. Few people have ever been treated more unfairly than Joseph was when his employer, Potiphar, threw him in jail as a result of the lies of Potiphar's wife.

Joseph's job as steward of Potiphar's house ended in disaster even though he had committed himself to serving Potiphar well. In the providence of God, however, Joseph's firing was only one step to being promoted to governor of all Egypt. The same providence guides your life and mine if we are God's servants.

For Individuals or Groups

1. Give an example of a time you or someone you know was treated unfairly at work.

2. What various forms can unfair treatment take? Give examples.

3. Why is poor treatment of employees by management shortsighted (p. 73)? How could this fact be communicated effectively to managers to help bring about change?

4. How else can management be encouraged to maintain healthy relationships with employees?

5. On pages 73-74 we read that stealing, a work slowdown or intentionally poor performance are not appropriate responses to unfair treatment. Do you

78

think there is a time when such a response might be called for? Explain.

6. Summarize in one sentence the six steps suggested in response to unfair treatment at work. How realistic and helpful do you think each step is? What other possible options would you add?

7. If there are no established grievance procedures (p. 76), what should an employee do?

8. When do you think keeping records (pp. 76-77) and putting complaints in writing is appropriate? When would it not be appropriate?

9. If you have a complaint at work, what next step could you take to begin to resolve it?

7

Loving
a Difficult
Coworker

• • • • • • • •

*M**ary likes almost everything about her job at a gift* shop: her part-time hours, the quality merchandise, the interesting customers who come from all over the world—everything except working with Dolores.

Mary starts getting depressed Monday evening, because Tuesday and Wednesday are "Dolores days," when she has to work with the abrasive woman. Mary has tried to get her hours adjusted to avoid Dolores, but no one else wants to work with her either.

What does Dolores do that makes her so obnoxious? For starters, she doesn't know the merchandise and can't handle the cash register without making mistakes. She also talks continually (usually about all the clever things she has done and said, which gets old fast). No one can tell Dolores anything because she's quick to say she already knows it.

Most of the other employees hardly make any attempt to hide how much they detest Dolores. As a Christian, however, Mary struggles to demonstrate the love of Christ to Dolores. When the others talk about Dolores, Mary holds back. None of us is perfect, she thinks. Let's give this poor, unhappy woman some sympathy.

But when she has to work with Dolores, her kind, understanding attitude quickly gets swept away by hard reality: Dolores is simply insufferable.

Insufferable Types

Many kinds of behavior make people hard to work with. Do you know any of the following coworkers?

The Blame-Shifter. Whenever something goes wrong, he tries to blame others by making all kinds of disclaimers: "I said we shouldn't do that"; "It wasn't my idea"; "I didn't really want to, but so and so told me to."

The Bootlicker. She works very hard when the boss is watching, but when the boss leaves she goofs off. She may even go so far as to get other employees in trouble to make herself look good by comparison and to show the boss whose side she's on.

The "Christian" Who Is an Embarrassment. This person claims to be a Christian but freely uses vulgar language, gossips, sleeps around or steals from the company. Then there's the tough-skinned, overzealous Christian who makes a laughingstock of believers by preaching all the time and telling other employees what sinners they are.

The Slacker. Some workers don't. They don't work, that is.

They put in their time, draw their checks, but do as little as they possibly can. A first cousin of the slacker is the time-stealer, the employee who continually comes in late, extends breaks, spends lots of work time on personal matters, then leaves early. You may have trouble loving a slacker or time-stealer whose laziness creates extra work for you since you must finish what they didn't get done.

The Griper. No job is perfect, and some employees get stuck in a negative mindset about work conditions or supervisors. Continually listening to someone complain is wearisome; and when you have to work with a griper, keeping a good attitude toward your own work may grow difficult.

The Foul-mouthed. Gutter talk, dirty jokes, profanity and vulgarisms flow from some people like dirty water in a storm sewer. It is language you neither use nor want to listen to, but they brazenly make it a part of your daily work environment.

The Repeller. An individual you would ordinarily avoid close contact with may be assigned to work with you. Perhaps he has offensive breath or body odor. Or perhaps he continually pollutes your air with cigarette smoke or makes you suffer through his other bad habits.

The Hateful. She might be subtly malignant and simply make you feel uncomfortable, or outright venomous and leave no doubt that she despises you or others and will do what she can to cause injury.

The Otherwise Obnoxious. Various other behaviors can make people difficult to work with. Dependent types may hang on you like a puppy dog. Domineering types may give you unwanted advice and insist you do things their way, even though they have no authority over you. Others may bore you to death with incessant chatter, always want to borrow money, try to drag you

83

into petty office politics, sexually harass you or put you down constantly.

Bearing with It

Face it. You will probably always have to work with problem people. Although we have described quite a few insufferable types, I'm sure we haven't covered them all. And forgive me for also mentioning the possibility, however remote, that you may also bug some people.

The Bible talks about something called forbearance precisely because we so easily get annoyed with each other. Paul admonished the Ephesians and the Colossians to bear with one another in love (see Eph 4:2; Col 3:13). That means we should accept one another, bad traits and all.

God himself has modeled extreme forbearance for us. He is holy and pure and exalted, while we are sometimes vile, petty and mean. Yet he loves us extravagantly. We honor and reflect our heavenly Father when we try to bear with people's failings.

Consider that people at work who bug you represent opportunities for you to practice forbearance. Is the grace of God operating in your life? If so, God's grace is as sufficient for you to endure a difficult coworker as it was for Paul to endure a chronic physical ailment he called a "thorn in my flesh" (see 2 Cor 12:7-9).

Recognize Your Limits

Knowing God's grace to be sufficient is one thing; overestimating your human limits is another. Mary, for example, felt guilty—not because she wasn't trying to show Christ's love to Dolores, but because she did not like the woman and found herself trying to put distance between them.

84

If we distance ourselves from troublesome people, it may seem we are admitting defeat. Shouldn't we involve ourselves in their lives as vibrant examples of God's power and expect that Christ will change them?

Not necessarily.

Everyone we touch will not be won, either to Christ or to be our friend. Everyone Jesus touched did not glorify God. On one occasion, Jesus healed ten lepers, but only one came back to give him thanks and experience spiritual transformation (see Luke 17:11-19).

We sometimes think that if we show the love of Christ to people, they will surely change. When we think this way, our "faith" may actually be arrogance. We're assuming, in effect, that we should be able to change people more effectively than Jesus did!

This faulty expectation sets us up for guilt when we "fail." When the nine lepers did not return to give thanks to Jesus, do you suppose he asked himself in great anguish, "Where did I fail?"

No. He realized that one leper was fertile soil for the kingdom of God and that the other nine were not—at least, not right then.

Our job is not to convert people. Our job is to love them. Love doesn't always give people what they want. So, despite your efforts, some coworkers will prefer to use, manipulate, intimidate or simply dislike you. If you honestly wish your fellow workers well, pray for them sincerely and make yourself available to them when they genuinely need you, then you are living in love. You don't have to let them mistreat you continually.

In Mary's case, Dolores showed no openness to Christ's love at all. She continued to blame others and justify herself in every situation. So Mary came to a few conclusions. First, no one could help Dolores until she wanted help, which would require that she acknowledge some need. Second, Mary was not responsible to save or change Dolores, but simply to guard her own attitude and remain available to God. Third, putting up with Dolores' obnoxious behavior did not help anyone. In the end, Mary decided to distance herself from Dolores, dealing with her lovingly but firmly as each situation demanded.

Someone has said that God can use anyone for some good purpose—even the most troublesome people can provide excellent examples of what not to become. A fellow worker who irritates you can serve you in just that way. God could hardly say more eloquently, "See how his behavior makes everyone, including himself, miserable. Make certain you never become like that." Believing that you can learn something even from those who bug you most can go a long way toward helping you cope.

A good sense of humor can also help you keep perspective. When Mary described to her family how Dolores would say, "Oh, I knew that" every time someone tried to tell her something, they decided to help her laugh about it. From time to time when Mary would correct someone at home, the standard response (with a mischievous grin) became, "Oh, I knew that!" Everyone would have a good laugh, and the tension Mary had brought home with her would dissolve.

A Word to the Hurting
Perhaps you identify more with Dolores than with Mary. You may not share all Dolores's characteristics, but you still feel like everyone at work dislikes or excludes you. When you try to make friends, they don't respond.

It's difficult in such a situation to evaluate whether or how much you are at fault. You may be asking yourself, "Do I have bad breath?" But the real question—What about my personality turns others off?—may be too painful to face. Dolores, for example, has never had the courage to ask why she turns people away. And so she goes on, hurting and being hurt, slowly becoming a bitter old woman.

If you feel generally disliked, that doesn't mean that you are a horrible person. Some comparatively small but significant changes in how you speak and relate to others could make a big difference.

We have described in this chapter some of the behaviors that bug people. Use those descriptions to take a personal inventory. Do not just glance over them and assume they do not apply to you. Pray over them and ask the Holy Spirit to open your eyes to any changes you need to make.

You might also go to a pastor or respected friend and ask for an evaluation of your behavior at certain points. Don't do so, however, if you can't hear criticism without becoming insulted, angry and defensive. That would be unfair to the one whose counsel you seek and it would do you no good.

When a person can't get along with others, self-centeredness in some form usually lies at the heart of the problem. You cannot overcome the problem of self-centeredness simply by asking God for strength to consider him and others more important than yourself. That is treating symptoms. What you need is to be radically changed inside so as to "think of yourself with sober judgment" (Rom 12:3). For help in getting a realistic view of how you should see yourself in relation to God and others, read my book *A True View of You*.[1]

Overcoming self-centeredness will inevitably help you both

relate to difficult coworkers better and become a more pleasant person to work with yourself. That's absolutely essential if you are trying to live out God's will. As Scripture puts it, "If it is possible, as far as it depends on you, live at peace with everyone" (Rom 12:18).

For Individuals or Groups

1 What kinds of problems have you had with coworkers?

2. The author lists a variety of "insufferable types" on pages 82-84. Why do people act in these ways?

3. What does it mean to forbear with others (p. 84)?

4. How has God shown forbearance with us?

5. Almost everyone of us knows someone who rubs us a little bit the wrong way. What could you do this week to reach out positively to such a person?

6. How can making more realistic expectations of others help us (pp. 84-86)? Do you think that to "recognize our limits" is actually an admission that there are situations God can't change? Explain.

7. Have you ever felt like you were "the problem coworker," the one others had trouble getting along with? What was it like?

8. What can you do to help make sure you are not the cause of a bad relationship?

8

Making a Boring Job Interesting

· · · · · · · · ·

*I*n their hearts people know *that work should be fun,*" *writes* John Naisbitt in *Reinventing the Corporation,* his upbeat analysis of future trends in the workplace.[1]

Wait a second. Work should be *fun?* That sounds a little idealistic, doesn't it? If work should be fun, something is certainly wrong with the job scene millions of us have known most of our lives.

Many people literally hate their jobs. I'm not talking about mild dissatisfaction; even people who love their jobs have off days. I'm not talking about fatigue, either. Everyone needs time off. I'm talking about people who every day dread going to boring or tedious jobs.

Boring Jobs I Have Known

I have worked at my share of monotonous jobs. I know how unpleasant a boring task can be, but I've also learned how you can actually turn job boredom to your advantage.

At one point in my life I spent many eight-hour shifts doing nothing but cutting wing slots in the sticks that became the fuselages of windup, rubber-band-powered toy airplanes. And that was one of my more exciting responsibilities. Far worse was a day of picking those same dyed sticks out of a jumbled heap and arranging them neatly in boxes. I did my share of that too. Not only did it bore me, but the dye and the dust got all over my hands and arms and made me itch.

At that time I felt demeaned by working at a toy factory. When people asked where I was employed, I answered, "A-J Aircraft Company," hoping I might not have to tell them the A-J stood for American Junior and that the aircraft we made were thirty-nine-cent balsa wood toys. Since then, however, I've found that "real men's work" can be just as monotonous. Making real-life instruments for real-life planes is unrelieved tedium when you drill holes in stainless steel plates all day.

Digging ditches is boring and hard labor besides. Long-haul driving can be boring too, especially through states where even the "scenic routes" only boast a tree or two. Then there's washing dishes in a restaurant. Or putting data in a processor all day. The list of potentially boring jobs goes on and on.

Of course, any job—whether monotonous or exciting—serves God if we do it in obedience to him. But even if we are consciously trying to glorify God in our work (as we discussed in chapter three), repetitive jobs may bore us because they offer no mental challenge. The worker operates on automatic pilot. Nevertheless, you can take what may be the worst aspect of your

90

job, boredom, and turn it into a benefit.

How? By taking advantage of those eight hours each day when your mind runs at idle. Those hours can do double duty for you. You can get paid for your physical labor or presence on the job while engaging in your own mental pursuits.

Here are some of the good things that others and I have extracted from otherwise boring jobs.

Spiritual Growth

The Bible says, "Do not let this Book of the Law depart from your mouth; meditate on it day and night, so that you may be careful to do everything written in it. Then you will be prosperous and successful" (Josh 1:8).

Few people can obey this admonition better than someone in a boring job. Those with challenging work which demands their full attention actually have forty hours a week less to meditate and pray than you do.

Many Christians have difficulty finding a few minutes each day to spend quietly before the Lord. I am one of those. I tend to get going as soon as I'm awake in the morning. Sometimes I am walking out the door to get started at something while still buttoning my shirt.

When I worked for A-J Aircraft, however, I spent hours at a time praying and meditating on Scripture. I reviewed Bible verses I'd memorized, taking time to dwell on the meaning of those verses and to think about how I should apply them to my life.

Ray Jossi, a Greyhound bus driver, turned boredom to his spiritual benefit too. Ray copes with and actually profits from the boredom of his job in two ways. First, he memorizes Scripture. Though he is now fifty-eight years old (some say older

91

people can't memorize well), Ray has learned fifty new verses within the last year. While driving he both learns new verses and reviews old ones, to keep them clear in his memory.

Ray also spends much time praying (with his eyes wide open, of course!). He doesn't just toss a quick, "God bless everybody" heavenward. Instead he has created a well-defined prayer list that he works through. After spending time praising and thanking the Lord, he prays for his immediate family. Then he prays for his extended family. Next he prays for a "critical list" of urgent problems. Fourth, he prays for all Christian pastors, beginning with his own. Finally, he prays for missionaries, including those he helps support.

The Bible says, "Do not be overcome by evil, but overcome evil with good" (Rom 12:21). Boredom very well may open the door to a sinful fantasy life. When you use a boring situation to grow spiritually rather than yield to temptation, you turn the tables on Satan and fulfill God's admonition to overcome evil with good.

Planning Sessions

A monotonous job can allow you to channel mental energy not only toward spiritual growth but also toward planning after-hours activities.

Among the beneficiaries of my boring job at A-J Aircraft were the junior boys I taught at Sunday school. It takes some planning to keep one step ahead of fourth- to sixth-grade boys and even more to exert a genuine spiritual influence on them. Much of my lesson preparation took place at work.

Similarly, during my ditch digging days our church, having moved to a new location, needed someone to spearhead a neighborhood outreach. I composed a survey we could use to find out more about people, mapped out our approach and devised a record-keeping system of new contacts—all in my head during work hours! The pastor and board liked my plan. A few weeks later, our members were canvassing the neighborhood, meeting our neighbors to let them know we cared and building a card file of names. A more challenging job would not have freed me to brainstorm that church visitation program.

Enhanced Creativity

People speak of being trapped in a boring job as if it were a prison. If you feel trapped in your job, remember that prison was the setting in which some of the great creative works of our age were born. Cheryl Forbes writes:

> It seems as if the greater the physical confinement the larger the imaginative space grows. John Bunyan and Alexander Solzhenitsyn are two examples. *Pilgrim's Progress* was written in prison, a tremendous feat. Greater still was that of Solzhenitsyn, who wrote in prison despite the fact that he was allowed no paper. He wrote in his head and memorized what he wrote. . . . Prison stripped him of everything except his imagination.[2]

You need not be a writer to use work time creatively. Forbes also tells how she turned her own job as a file clerk into something more:

> As much as I wanted to make the job itself a work of imagination, I could never find a way to do it. However, the time was never wasted; a person can file quite well and do many other things, such as writing or planning a party or organizing the rest of your work schedule. Remember Einstein's job at the patent office. In his later years he was grateful he had had such a routine job for it freed his mind to fly to the

problems of quanta, light particles, and relativity. Enforced, unimaginative work is not always bad. It can be a mental vacation.[3]

Job Enrichment

So far we have been talking about taking advantage of a boring job to embark on interesting and worthwhile mental flights elsewhere. Sometimes, however, our job itself conceals interesting elements we have simply never seen.

Too often we are like the shepherd who one day came across a botanist on a mountain slope. The botanist was studying the ground closely with a large magnifying glass.

"What are you doing?" the shepherd asked.

"I'm studying these enchanting blooms," said the botanist.

"Blooms?" the shepherd echoed. "There are no flowers around here."

"But of course there are," said the botanist. "Come, see for yourself."

The shepherd peered through the magnifying glass at delicate white-petaled, pink-centered flowers. "They're beautiful!" he murmured. Then he exclaimed, "Why, they're all over here! There must be a million of them!"

When at last he returned the glass to the botanist, the shepherd had tears in his eyes. "To think," he said, "that I have been trampling these flowers under my feet for years and never saw them."

You may be convinced that there are no unseen, unappreciated flowers on your job, and perhaps you are right. But don't be too sure. At least take a look. Ask the Lord for a magnifying glass that will let you see clearly.

Telephone operators at Pacific Bell, for instance, discovered their jobs held more interest than they thought. Most of the seventeen thousand operators had found little challenge in putting through calls or giving out phone numbers all day. Then Pacific Bell hired Timothy Gallwey, who sets up employee training programs for major corporations. Pacific Bell wanted to increase operator efficiency and courtesy and reduce missed work days. Gallwey said he could achieve that by reducing job boredom.

Gallwey helped the operators focus attention on the one element they dealt with continually—callers. He trained the operators to listen not only to what was said, but to the voices themselves. Were they relaxed or stressed? Angry or warm? Slurred or lively?

Operators began to recognize how much they could tell about a person just by the tone of voice and manner of speaking. They also realized what a great asset this skill could be to them off the job, helping them tune in to family members, friends and even to their own moods.

Eventually the operators could not only detect customers' attitudes but also affect their attitudes for the better. Irritated callers would warm up noticeably when answered with a friendly voice. The operators had discovered a fascinating and very useful element of their work.

Preparing for Something Better

As we have discussed, seemingly unchallenging jobs have their merits. Still, if your work bores you, God may be prodding you to look for more interesting work.

You could argue, in fact, that God never intended people to work at boring jobs. Can you picture Adam or Eve off in some corner of Eden spending day after day doing nothing but cutting slots in sticks? The industrial revolution produced a higher standard of living materially, but it did so at the cost of placing many people in unfulfilling jobs.

Changing jobs scares us for a number of reasons. For one, although you know the bad things about your present job, a new job that looks better could turn out worse. For another, even if the job does prove better, you might not be able to do it well. You could end up with no job at all.

Although you don't want to act on impulse and regret it later, you shouldn't let such fears paralyze you as they did the unfaithful servant. Jesus condemned him for burying his talent in fear that he would lose out in the end (see Mt 25:24-30).

If you are currently employed, you don't have to rush into a new job because of economic necessity. You can move ahead deliberately. Continue working at your present job while you take aptitude tests, get career guidance, do research, perhaps even work part time at other jobs you think you might like. In chapter twelve we will examine the subject of changing vocations in more detail.

Many lament the fact that they are too soon old and too late smart. Having failed to get a good education or a skill, they feel trapped in a boring, low-paying job. But wanting to get out of a boring job may provide just the motivation you need to get more training. It also may offer considerable time to work on studies. Many people have earned an academic degree while working in a position (such as security guard) that actually allows study during work hours or at least leaves the mind fresh for study during off hours.

Maybe it will take you eight years to get a degree you might have earned in four as a full-time student. Maybe you are saying, "By then I'll be forty years old (or fifty years old, or whatever).

But you are going to be forty years old whether you get a degree or not. Wouldn't you rather reach age forty qualified to take a more challenging job?

If you're stuck in a boring job, look to the God of wonders to help you do something about it. Maybe he will help you find new interest in your job. Maybe he will help you transform your workplace to a place where he meets with you daily. Maybe he will lead you out of your present job to a far better one.

Jesus said, "Ask and it will be given to you; seek and you will find; knock and the door will be opened to you" (Mt 7:7). This is a call, not to be passive, but to take action. Applied to your boring job or boring life, this principle of actively pursuing something better can quickly infuse your life with some exciting changes.

It's your move.

For Individuals or Groups

1. Almost every job has some parts of it that are drudgery. What are some of the boring aspects of your job?

2. How can you take advantage of the time during which your mind might otherwise be running in neutral?

3. Sometimes routine jobs (like performing certain accounting functions) don't allow your mind to be elsewhere while you do your work. How can boredom be overcome in these situations?

4. How else can creativity be put to work even in routine jobs (pp. 94-95)?

5. What advantages does a routine job have during off hours?

6. How is one's attitude key in dealing with boredom at work?

7. Is having a boring job a sufficient reason to consider changing jobs? Why or why not?

9

When Your Job
Is Hazardous
to Your Health

· · · · · · · ·

*E*ven as you read this, about four hundred fifty families in the United States are mourning a loved one accidentally killed on the job within the last month.

According to National Institute for Occupational Safety and Health statistics from 1980 to 1984, mining ranks as the most dangerous occupation, with thirty fatalities per year for each 100,000 workers. Construction came in second with twenty-three deaths a year for each 100,000 workers.

More Than Statistics

These numbers don't tell the whole story about safe work environments, of course; they only reflect on-the-job fatalities, not general health hazards.

I once worked as plant manager for an agricultural chemicals manufacturer. In those days no federal watchdog agency regulated hazards in the workplace, and I was regularly exposed to chemicals that kill insects.

"Not to worry," the owner of the plant told me. "It won't hurt you. My own blood is probably five per cent DDT by now and it hasn't hurt me yet."

One day the owner introduced a new pesticide. "This stuff is called TEPP," he said, "and unlike those other chemicals, this kills humans as well as insects, even if you don't swallow or inhale it. Like nerve gas, it goes right through your skin."

Soon I found myself wearing rubber gloves, tightfitting cuffs and a face mask to cope with TEPP. Even so, I had worked with TEPP only a couple of days when my vision suddenly blurred.

The next day I presented myself to the public health authorities in our county. Their tests confirmed that I had been poisoned by TEPP, though apparently not seriously.

"Who needs this?" I thought. In less than a week I had found a new job.

Professionals at Risk

Although a mine, construction site or chemical company might witness more accidents, many office jobs probably present at least as many health hazards, including the higher stress levels and more sedentary lifestyle they demand.

During a nine-month period in late 1986 and early 1987, for example, the presidents of ten large Japanese corporations died in office. Commenting on this, Dr. Kenshiro Ohara of Hamamatsu University Hospital compared Japanese industry to the Japanese army of World War 2. "One officer dies and they bring in another, and another, until the hill is finally won from the enemy. These men are really being killed in action."

Business executives all over the world have been "killed in action" by the stress of their jobs. (We will deal at length with stress and how to handle it in the next chapter.) Besides stress, most professional and white-collar workers face the side effects of a sedentary lifestyle.

Doctors tell us that a sedentary lifestyle will:

1. Increase both the likelihood and the severity of heart attacks or other cardiovascular disease.

2. Add to weight problems. Exercise plays as important a role as diet in keeping trim. And excess weight, in turn, contributes to poor physical and emotional health.

3. Contribute to poor muscle tone, a low energy level, bad posture and the resulting lower back pain or disability.

Besides stress and a sedentary lifestyle, white-collar workers usually run risks associated with working closely with other people in confined quarters—namely, the risk of contracting colds, influenza and even pneumonia. In addition, infectious agents in the walls, floors or air conditioning systems of even the most plush high-rise office building can make people sick.

Professionals such as police, lawyers, judges and psychologists who deal with disturbed or angry people take yet other risks. Not long ago my daughter-in-law Cindy, a mental-health case worker, faced a threat to her life when a client pulled a knife and tried to stab her. Cindy was able to escape because she had kept herself between her client and her office door (always a good idea). Later, the prosecutor at the woman's trial proved that she had tried to buy a gun earlier that day, but was put off by a five-day waiting period. Had she been able to buy the gun, Cindy might not be alive today.

Who Is Safe?

We have described the comparatively high risk of accidents on some blue-collar jobs. We have talked about harmful stress and the lack of needed physical exercise on white-collar jobs. We have cited the threat of personal attack on professionals. Isn't anybody safe?

Probably not. I asked Harold Allen, who for thirty years has pursued the risky vocation of cab driver, for his views on the relative risks of various jobs. "Aren't you afraid?" I asked him.

"No, a person can't live in fear," Harold said. "I've never been robbed or assaulted in all my years driving a cab, though I have known several who have. But, then, I also have an acquaintance who was robbed on her job in a music store, of all places. So where is a person safe? My trust is in the Lord."

Although each job carries risks, workers can diminish or increase the risks. Harold feels that because he has worked with the public for a long time, he has developed a sixth sense that tells him when something is wrong. "Little things tip me off," he said. "We drivers also have secret codes by which to alert our dispatcher when we suspect we may be in trouble. If I am very suspicious about a fare, I may suddenly drive into a place where there are lots of people and say, 'Okay, this is as far as we go. You don't owe me a cent, but this cab just became unavailable.' "

One Mistake

While years on the job can make one wise to the hazards, as Harold suggests, the same familiarity can also lead to careless, possibly fatal mistakes.

I still remember a fatality that occurred at the shipyard where I once worked. Eric, an electrician who had worked in the shipyard for twenty-five years, had been electrocuted just before my shift began. "He got into the 440," his coworkers told me, referring to the high tension 440-volt power lines that operated the overhead cranes.

I winced inwardly. Every day I began my shift near those same 440-volt lines. Part of my job as maintenance machinist was to climb up and grease the cranes.

No one seemed to know just how Eric had come into contact with the lines, but he had apparently gotten a bit careless after all the years he had worked close to them. One mistake was all it took.

Similarly, investigators of a recent airline crash, which killed the entire cockpit crew and many passengers, discovered that the flaps were not properly set for takeoff. Any novice pilot knows that setting the flaps is an essential basic procedure. Yet according to the investigators the veteran airline captain had somehow overlooked it.

Not Worth It

What significant health risks does your job bring? We each need to evaluate those risks, ask ourselves whether we are willing to pay the price our present jobs require of us, and consider what we can do to improve matters.

No job should require us to lose our lives or our health. Even the work of the gospel does not call us to self-destruct.

There used to be a popular saying among the students at my Bible college: "I would rather burn out for God than rust out." I never liked that saying. Why should I burn out by setting a furious pace or rust out by sitting idle? Why not wear out after many years of effective service? Although serving Christ may in some situations make us vulnerable to persecution or even endanger our lives, that's quite different from us knowingly abusing or endangering ourselves out of recklessness or ambition.

Robert Murray McCheyne burned out for God. McCheyne, a Scottish prodigy who matriculated from Edinburgh University in 1827 at age fourteen, became a licensed Presbyterian preacher at age twenty-two. A year later he was leading a congregation of eleven hundred.

McCheyne devoted himself to his work with such ardor that his health failed. Though he was much admired and later referred to as "the saintly McCheyne," he died at age twenty-nine, lamenting, "God gave me a message to deliver and a horse to ride. Alas, I have killed the horse and now I cannot deliver the message."

Overexertion does not glorify God. Our bodies are more than horses we ride to exhaustion or machines that can work overtime with no serious effects. Our bodies are temples of the Holy Spirit to be cared for and respected.

When our jobs excite and motivate us, however, we can easily risk emotional burnout and physical exhaustion without realizing it. We may need help to see that our lives have gotten out of balance.

Pause right now and take a good look at your job. Ask yourself, "What do I gain or expect to gain from this job?"

Most people would probably list material benefits (money to supply needs and wants), emotional benefits (self-respect, a sense of achievement) and social benefits (respect of other workers and the larger community). A Christian would also expect spiritual benefits (a sense that one is doing the will of God).

Now ask yourself, "Am I reaping these benefits and, if so, what is it costing me?"

Typically the cost will include a significant amount of time, energy and emotional commitment. So far, so good. But the cost can escalate dramatically if you don't watch it. Besides time, energy and commitment, the job may begin to exact your life-blood. Then the question becomes, "Does the cost outweigh the benefits?" Too many people have sacrificed their health (not to mention their families) for a career, only to sacrifice that career in a last-ditch effort to regain their well-being.

Options for Endangered Workers

What can you do if your job threatens your health? Consider these ideas:

1. *Terminate the hazard.* Instead of terminating your job, see if you can get rid of the hazard or at least reduce it to an acceptable level. If noise is damaging your hearing, for example, you could wear earplugs. In other situations, you may need to enlist other workers, negotiate with management or call in government agencies to initiate change.

Doing something to reduce hazards, rather than just quitting, may allow you to serve others' interests, as well as your own. If you walk off the job, the company will probably just hire someone else who will be subjected to the same risks. Though no one might expressly credit you for helping create a safer work environment for others, "God is not unjust; he will not forget your work and the love you have shown him as you have helped his people and continue to help them" (Heb 6:10).

2. *Quit without quitting.* Perhaps you can quit your job without leaving your employer. Could you change responsibilities or even move to another department?

Clint Palmer worked for many years in the auto paint shop of a major car dealership. Eventually he became so concerned about the health hazard of paint fumes that he considered quitting. Rather than let a good employee leave, the employer promoted him to service manager. He continued to work for the same company in a closely related field but no longer was exposed to the fumes emanating from the paint shop.

3. *Plan to change careers periodically.* Develop a mentality, an expectation from the start, that you will probably work in other fields during your lifetime. That way, if and when you do need to change jobs (for health or other reasons), it won't seem such a radical or impossible thing to do. I'm not suggesting that you should know exactly how long you will stay on your present job or what you will do next, but simply that you stay flexible.

A change of workplace periodically might do wonders for you emotionally and spiritually as well as physically. In chapter twelve we'll explore how to expand your world by breaking away from a comfortable but stifling job situation.

4. *Change your after-hours lifestyle.* You can eliminate or minimize some job-related health hazards by the lifestyle you choose off the job. If your work keeps you sitting all day, for example, you can walk, jog, swim, take an aerobics class or work out with weights to get your needed exercise off the job.

If your work creates stress for you, you can learn how to leave it behind when you go home. You can also learn relaxation techniques (detailed in the next chapter) to use both on and off the job.

Find rest and strength by spending free time with the Lord who invites you to come to him for solace anytime. Jesus said, "Come to me, all you who are weary and burdened, and I will give you rest. Take my yoke upon you and learn from me, for I am gentle and humble in heart, and you will find rest for your souls" (Mt 11:28-29).

You may find it especially helpful to pray for strength before the rush of your workday begins. "I rely so much on my morning time with the Lord," one executive told me. "It's great to go to work refreshed and encouraged, ready for the challenges of the day and fortified against temptation."

There's a Lion Outside!

Although dangers exist in the workplace, we can't let them immobilize us. Home can be dangerous too; more people die in bed than anywhere else!

Sometimes the supposed dangers of the workplace become an excuse for laziness. As the writer of Proverbs put it, "The sluggard says, 'There is a lion outside!' or, 'I will be murdered in the streets!' " (Prov 22:13).

To those tempted to be lazy I would say, forget about the lion outside (the exaggerated dangers of the workplace). The lion stalking you is "your enemy the devil" who "prowls around like a roaring lion looking for someone to devour" (1 Pet 5:8). Sloth is one of the seven deadly sins, so when the devil traps you in laziness, the lion already has you.

Hazards do exist in the workplace, and so do the remedies for those hazards, but the remedy is not idleness. God expects us to work.

For Individuals or Groups

1. What are some of the physical risks you face because of your work (even if you have a white-collar job)?

2. "Isn't anybody safe?" the author asks. Immediately he answers, "Probably not" (p. 102). How do you respond to the idea that no job will ever be completely risk free?

3. How should we balance the desire for safe working environments with the cost of eliminating all serious (even if unlikely) risks?

4. What benefits do you expect to reap from your job?

5. What are the costs associated in gaining those benefits?

6. How do you judge when the costs outweigh the benefits?

7. Do you think the gospel requires us to burn out rather than rust out (p. 103)? Explain.

8. Robert Murray McCheyne said, "God gave me a message to deliver and a horse to ride. Alas, I have killed the horse and now I cannot deliver the message" (p. 104). What does McCheyne seem to imply is more important than burning out for God?

9. What steps does the chapter suggest for dealing with job-related dangers (pp. 105-107)? Which step could help you deal with a risk you face?

10

Overcoming
Work-Related
Stress

· · · · · · · ·

*A*s we mentioned in the last chapter, even "safe" jobs can
exact a high toll from you if they make you work under stress.

Just what kind of high toll are we talking about? According
to Hans Selye, the medical doctor often called "the world's leading authority" on the subject, stress can age you prematurely
and it can contribute to high blood pressure, heart attack, ulcers
and mental illness.

Working under stress is also no fun.

To be more specific, *negative* stress is what does all the dirty
work. Selye terms this *distress*. In his book *Stress without Distress*, Selye says, in essence, that fulfilling work involves a positive kind of stress: "Successful activity, no matter how intense,

leaves you with comparatively few such scars. . . . On the contrary, it provides you with the exhilarating feeling of youthful strength, even at a very advanced age. Work wears you out mainly through the frustration of failure."[1]

In other words, you need to work at a job that is right for you. In Selye's words, you should "select an environment . . . which is in line with your innate preferences—to find an activity which you like and respect. Only thus can you eliminate the need for frustrating constant readaptation that is the major cause of distress."[2]

To put it another way, if you want to avoid a lot of damaging stress, you must *take this job and love it.* That is not just a clever title. It is a prescription for health, long life and happiness.

I think of Mike Donahue, an acquaintance of mine who is a television news anchorman. There is considerable stress to his job with its continual sense of urgency, its drama and tight deadlines. Yet Mike loves it. He is following the counsel of his father, who years ago told him in regard to choosing a vocation, "Son, find something you'd rather do than play." It was homespun advice, but it squares well with the conclusions Dr. Selye has reached through forty years of research.

Psychologist Susan Seliger offers further insight into how a job that is not right for us causes damaging stress:

The source of chronic stress can be found not so much in what we do each day but how we feel about it. Police officers, for example, complain that they experience more stress handling boring paperwork than they do while making arrests or responding to crimes in progress. They were trained to act, not sit and write, and that is what they feel competent doing. If we sense that we are not entirely in control of our lives, and every little move makes us anxious or dissatisfied and

110

sends out a stress alarm, then we are never allowing ourselves the chance to say "Whew" and recuperate. It's the buildup of small but constant stress responses, not the occasional big ones, that inflicts the most bodily harm.[3]

In Search of Solutions

Here are some solutions for dealing with job-related stress.

1. *Work to the glory of God.* Apart from choosing the right job, doing your work to God's glory will go further toward eliminating job distress than anything else you can do. In chapter three we described the elements involved in working to the glory of God (as summarized on p. 42). Dr. Selye, in his book, prescribes various antidotes to distress. A remarkable correlation exists between these two lists.

Trace it with me.

First, we said our work glorifies God when we do it as an act of obedience. God himself will recognize and reward such work. "Whatever you do, work at it with all your heart, as working for the Lord, not for men, since you know that you will receive an inheritance from the Lord as a reward. It is the Lord Christ you are serving" (Col 3:23-24).

Note how this corresponds with the following from Dr. Selye: "Man must have recognition; he cannot tolerate constant censure, for that is what—more than any other stressor—makes work frustrating and harmful."[4]

When we work to the glory of God, we have his personal assurance that he recognizes and will reward our work.

Second, we said our work glorifies God when it is performed in a spirit of service to others. Dr. Selye alludes to this aspect of work when he writes, "For many older people . . . the most difficult aspect of retirement to bear is the feeling of being

111

useless."[5] He also writes that he himself had been "so fascinated by the possibilities of research on life and disease" that from age eighteen he had put in extremely long days, yet suffered little distress. "Now at the age of sixty-seven, I still get up at four or five o'clock in the morning and still work until six at night, with few interruptions; and I am still perfectly happy leading this kind of life. No regrets."[6]

Being useful, researching disease in order to help people— these are expressions of a spirit of service, and they help make job stress positive.

Third, we said our work glorifies God when we do it with a spirit of thankfulness and gratitude to the Lord. Dr. Selye writes: "Among all the emotions, those that—more than any others— account for the absence or presence of harmful stress (distress) in human relations are the feelings of gratitude and goodwill and their negative counterparts, hatred with the urge for revenge."[7]

If you want to work without harmful stress, your bitterness, anger and resentment will have to go. Choose feelings of gratitude and goodwill instead. If that seems impossible, go back and read again the story of Glen Thornton and of Joseph (p. 39-40).

Fourth, our work glorifies God when it reflects his workmanship and excellence. Dr. Selye writes, "I would say that, among people engaged in the most common occupations of modern society . . . one of the major sources of distress arises from dissatisfaction with life, namely, from disrespect for their own accomplishments." He goes on to write of man's need "to satisfy his innate urge for self-expression—to complete whatever he considers his mission, whatever tasks he feels he has been built to perform. This rule again is not merely born out of man's imagination or some artificially rationalized code; it is the manifestation of a deep-rooted natural law."[8]

The above-described correlation between Dr. Selye's stress studies and my study of working to the glory of God seems significant. When independent studies reach similar conclusions, it adds weight to the validity of those conclusions, especially when the approach to the issues has been totally different, as in this case.

It should come as no surprise to us that working to the glory of God reduces stress. Jesus said as much: "Come to me, all you who are weary and burdened, and I will give you rest. Take my yoke upon you and learn from me, for I am gentle and humble in heart, and you will find rest for your souls. For my yoke is easy and my burden is light" (Mt 11:28-30).

Besides handling distress by the most basic expedient of working to the glory of God, here are some further suggestions for dealing with job-related stress.

2. *Lighten up*. When I feel stressed, nothing irritates me more than someone who breezily says, "Lighten up. Don't take it so seriously."

If I am groaning inside, frustrated by an overwhelming task, I don't want to hear somebody who feels none of my pain suggest that I change my attitude. If I were at all given to violence, you could hardly say anything that would make me more likely to punch you in the nose than "Lighten up!"

Therefore, I am not suggesting that you simply laugh it off when you are caught in a stressful job situation. Rather, you should cultivate light-heartedness in your life as a whole. If you are by nature an intense person, you may need to give yourself permission to relax. Intense Christians tend to believe, falsely, that they must take life by the throat and extract from it as much as possible.

But, you might retort, what about Scripture passages such as the following:

Therefore, my dear brothers, stand firm. Let nothing move you. Always give yourselves fully to the work of the Lord, because you know that your labor in the Lord is not in vain. (1 Cor 15:58)

Be very careful, then, how you live—not as unwise but as wise, making the most of every opportunity, because the days are evil. (Eph 5:15-16)

As long as it is day, we must do the work of him who sent me. Night is coming, when no one can work. (Jn 9:4)

Whatever your hand finds to do, do it with all your might. (Eccl 9:10)

Of course we should work heartily and diligently as these verses exhort us. However, they only represent part of the picture. Some Christians tend to forget about soothing passages such as these:

You will keep in perfect peace him whose mind is steadfast, because he trusts in you. (Is 26:3)

Do not fret—it leads only to evil. (Ps 37:8)

Cast all your anxiety on [God] because he cares for you. (1 Pet 5:7)

Of course, if you feel lighthearted because you're refusing to assume responsibility or take life seriously, you don't need exhortations to relax. You need to heed biblical passages that admonish us to serve God earnestly. But if you're headed toward ulcers and high blood pressure, you must accept Scripture's commands to let go.

3. *Compartmentalize your life.* You can also reduce job-related stress by compartmentalizing your life.

By "compartmentalizing" I don't mean separating your work

114

from your faith. Rather, I mean allotting certain hours to work and certain hours to other activities.

As we said before, God apparently intended for Adam and Eve to work and to relax. God placed Adam "in the Garden of Eden to work it and take care of it" (Gen 2:15). But God also came "walking in the garden in the cool of the day," to fellowship with Adam after the day's work was done (Gen 3:8). God also established the Sabbath as a day of rest: "Six days you shall labor and do all your work, but the seventh day is a Sabbath to the LORD your God. On it you shall not do any work" (Ex 20:9-10).

God knows that we need rest from the stress of our jobs. When we take work home and allow it to occupy our minds during time allotted for rest, we violate the spirit of the sabbath. We also invite fatigue. Life becomes a drag, and we identify with the worker who remarked, "You know, I have been working all my life, but somehow it seems longer."

Attitudes and Actions

4. *Become more aware of your body.* In addition to reducing or preventing stress, you can also physically counteract it. That is, you can reduce the damaging effects of work-related stress if you learn to relax your body. Strenuous physical activity such as running or aerobics releases tension. So does milder exercise such as walking or swimming. You can also learn how to relax right on the job.

Don was having such severe backaches that he at last agreed to see a doctor. After a thorough examination, the doctor assured Don that nothing was wrong physically. "It's tension," the doctor said. "I can give you some muscle relaxant, but that won't get to the cause of the problem. You need to learn how to relax."

"Tension?" Don thought. "This doctor doesn't know what he's talking about. I'm not tense."

The backaches continued, and eventually Don decided to try the doctor's relaxation technique. "I want you to put this in your schedule at least once every two hours," the doctor had said. He told Don to relax his whole body by concentrating on one area at a time. Starting with his hands and arms, Don would tense every muscle tightly for a moment, then relax it. Next, he would do the same with his shoulders and the muscles across his upper back. Then he would tense his abdomen and relax it. Finally, he would flex his legs, his feet and his toes, almost as if he were stretching.

Don was surprised to discover how tense he was each time he began the relaxation exercise. Consciously relaxing not only cured his backaches, but energized him all day.

Taking care of your body by relaxing, exercising, eating right and drinking plenty of liquids (preferably water) will help dissipate stress. While bad work situations can be hard on your health, poor health also makes you more vulnerable to bad work situations.

5. *Work efficiently without hurrying.* Hurry is a tense state of mind. You can work productively without hurrying—and, on the other hand, you can hurry without getting much done.

When you feel pressure to hurry, remind yourself that you can do almost as much work (and sometimes more) without a heavy injection of mental distress. Make a rule: I will hurry only in emergencies.

6. *Consider the cost-effectiveness of stressed job performance.* You may be able to do some tasks more quickly if you get keyed up. If you pay a high price in terms of well-being for a small gain in performance, however, you have been foolish.

Efficiency-minded people (like me) who search for every possible way to save money and time have the most difficulty accepting this. One hot day, for instance, I needed a stick of margarine and opened the refrigerator to get it. Without really thinking about it, I tried to pull a stick from an already opened carton to avoid standing in front of the refrigerator with the door ajar (which wastes energy) while I opened a carton and got the margarine.

Well, the stick would not readily slip out of the already-opened carton. I know this sounds silly, but I began to get flustered. I realized that if I didn't get the stick out quickly and shut the door, I would waste more energy than if I had pulled out the whole carton, removed a stick, and then returned the carton (which would require opening the door twice.)

That's when I realized how stressed out I was—all to save a penny or less by having that door open for a total of 4.2 seconds instead of 5.9 seconds. Meanwhile, my blood pressure was probably rising drastically and my nerves were becoming frayed. The amount of stress I was putting myself through was hardly cost-effective.

In the midst of a harried workday, periodically ask yourself whether the amount of stress you are bringing to your job is producing a corresponding improved productivity. Then even if it is, try to work smarter instead of harder.

7. *Seek diversions.* As much as you can, try to vary work tasks so that they suit your changing aptitudes and energy levels. Dr. Selye writes, "In stress research, we have found that, when completion of one particular task becomes impossible, diversion, a voluntary change of activity, is frequently as good as—if not better than—a rest."[9]

Routine work can be a relief from creative or intellectually demanding work. Physical labor can be a welcome change from mental exertion. If your job doesn't allow you much latitude for variety, at least try to counterbalance work responsibilities with very different leisure activities.

8. *Lean on God.* To minimize stress, you need to follow the many biblical principles that encourage us ultimately to give our cares and anxieties to the Lord. Cultivate that lively trust in God that enables you to rely on your relationship with him rather than your job performance for meaning.

John Greenleaf Whittier expressed in poetry a prayer we need to make our own when work-related stress threatens to overwhelm us.

Dear Lord and Father of mankind,
Forgive our foolish ways.
Reclothe us in our rightful mind;
In purer lives thy service find,
In deeper reverence, praise.

Drop thy still dews of quietness,
Till all our strivings cease;
Take from our souls the strain and stress,
And let our ordered lives confess
The beauty of thy peace.

For Individuals or Groups

1. What kinds of stress do you face on the job?

2. Is stress always negative or destructive? Explain.

3. Psychologist Susan Seliger is quoted as saying, "The source of chronic stress can be found not so much in what we do each day but how we feel about it" (p. 110). Do you agree that our environment does not cause us stress so much as we create the stress internally? Explain.

4. How can working to the glory of God actually help reduce stress (pp. 111-

118

13)?

5. Is lightheartedness contrary to the seriousness with which Scripture says we are to take God's commands for our lives (pp. 113-14)?

6. What are the benefits of paying attention to your body in relieving stress (pp. 115-16).

7. The chapter also lists working efficiently without hurrying, counting the cost of certain tasks, seeking diversions and leaning on God (pp. 116-18). Which of these is most helpful to you in dealing with stress?

8. What else have you found helpful?

9. What one step can you take this week to reduce the stress in your life?

11

Are You a
Workaholic?

• • • • • • • •

*M*any people serve their vocations with a devotion due
only to God. It is one thing to do our work heartily as unto the
Lord; it is quite another to sell our souls to the workplace.

In the previous two chapters we talked about jobs that demand too much physically or emotionally. Now let's examine
how jobs may also drain us spiritually by demanding a high level
of commitment that crowds out God and others.

Who Makes the Demands?

"You don't want to go to work for that publisher," a friend told
me when I was considering a job change. "They pay well, but
they also think they own you. They're one of those high-pressure

outfits that expects managers to eat, breathe and sleep nothing else but the job."

Some employers are like that: intense workaholics who expect their salaried workers to follow suit. They may even take pride in their single-minded devotion to the job.

It makes me think of the car maker who advertised: "We are driven!"

I inwardly replied, "I hope not. Cars should be driven, but people should not."

Many workaholics, however, drive themselves without any pressure from management. Some inner need—perhaps to earn self-worth through achievements, perhaps to compensate for loneliness or failure in other areas of life—compels them to work, work, work. People in the workaholic's life who don't affirm him apart from his achievements may contribute to his compulsion.

This consuming need to focus all of one's life on work belies a spiritual problem. As Christians, we believe that God, who ultimately provides for our needs, created us for more than work. We don't need to labor constantly, acting as if everything hinges on our efforts, because God has already given us salvation, peace and dignity—which we could never earn. He declares us worthy of his love whether we feel worthwhile or not.

Working Too Hard

Recently I conducted a seminar for Christians in the secular workplace. Several participants affirmed that we need to "do our best" on the job. Though I understood what they meant, that kind of statement may encourage a workaholic who sincerely believes she is only doing "her best" when she keeps working too hard.

How hard should we work, then? Scripture gives some rather clear guidelines. We are working too hard whenever:

1. *Our job becomes more important to us than the Lord.* The first of the Ten Commandments reads, "You shall have no other gods before me" (Ex 20:3). Anything that takes first place in our lives takes the place that belongs to God.

But, you may ask, if God commands us to work and our work serves him (as we said in chapters one and three), how can it at the same time be an act of idolatry?

Keep in mind the important distinction between means and ends. God has ordained work (as well as music, relationships and art) as a means to worship and serve him. But when we make any of God's good gifts an end in itself, it becomes idolatrous. We begin to glorify that gift or ourselves, rather than God. Worshipful music, for example, beautifully reflects God's glory. Some musicians, however, love music so much that it becomes an end in itself. Other gifted performers no doubt begin to live for the public adulation they receive on stage. Either way, God gets crowded out.

Pretend you are an unseen observer in the Garden of Eden. Adam and Eve have not yet eaten the forbidden fruit. They are cultivating the garden as God commanded them. And they are loving it.

Adam and Eve plan to use the creativity God has given them to develop the garden. They will place a bridge here, divert part of the stream to make a pool there, even build an observation platform in a tree. On this particular day Adam and Eve are busily engaged in their stream diversion project. They have been working for weeks and now very soon will flood the hollow where their pool will be.

The sun is low. Soon the Lord God will be walking in the

123

garden to meet with them in the cool of the day. But Adam can only think about how close they are to finishing. He can't wait to see the water run down and create the new pool!

Adam takes a quick glance at the setting sun and knows it's time to meet with God. "I can't leave now!" he thinks, and keeps working.

It's a conscious choice, and yet it isn't. Adam is so wrapped up in tending the garden (as God commanded him) that he scarcely recognizes what is happening. The creation—the garden with all its delights—is crowding out the Creator. Adam won't have time to fellowship with God today. He has to work.

Jesus warned about the danger of earthly concerns crowding God out of our lives: "Still others, like seed sown among thorns, hear the word; but the worries of this life, the deceitfulness of wealth and the desires for other things come in and choke the word, making it unfruitful" (Mk 4:18-19).

Unfortunately, good things such as work can usurp the place of God in our lives without our realizing it. If we are so busy working that we have no time or energy for prayer, Bible study, meditation, fellowship or worship, we should acknowledge that our lives have grown dangerously unbalanced.

2. *Our job becomes more important to us than family.* We must not give to our jobs the time, energy and interest that belong to our families. This means we must take time to nurture our children as Scripture admonishes us (see Eph 6:4). It also means we must set aside unhurried time for loving involvement, including sexual relations, with our husband or wife (see 1 Cor 7:3-5).

3. *Our job demands too many hours.* Well, you might ask, how many hours are too many?

No one can lay down strict guidelines as to how many hours

a Christian should work. But if your work schedule does not allow time for family and other activities, you're working too hard. Friends, rest, recreation and educational activities deserve our time as well. As the psalmist put it, "In vain you rise early and stay up late, toiling for food to eat—for he grants sleep to those he loves" (Ps 127:2).

Your work hours should reflect your personal energy level. Although the standard work week in the United States is forty hours, that does not suit all people at all times. Still, if you regularly work much more than forty hours a week, you might at least question whether you should slow down.

4. *Our work pace destroys our health.* As we said in the previous two chapters, a job that endangers our health demands too much. No job should continually wear us down physically. Scripture teaches that our bodies are temples of the Holy Spirit for which we are responsible: "Don't you know that you yourselves are God's temple and that God's Spirit lives in you? If anyone destroys God's temple, God will destroy him; for God's temple is sacred, and you are that temple" (1 Cor 3:16-17).

Not Working Hard Enough
Scripture also instructs us to work diligently. We are not working hard enough when:

1. *We are not applying ourselves.* God wants us to put ourselves into our work: "Whatever you do, work at it with all your heart, as working for the Lord, not for men" (Col 3:23).

2. *We don't care about the quality of our work.* Whenever an employer hires us to do something, we become stewards of his resources (money, equipment, office space and company reputation, to name a few). As Christians, we please God when we treat our employer with respect by using those resources wisely

to produce quality work. As Paul reminds us, "It is required that those who have been given a trust must prove faithful" (1 Cor 4:2).

The Choice

As you evaluate your job's demands by these standards, you may feel that your career advancement or even your job security requires that you work far harder than we've indicated you should. Perhaps you are right. David Ogilvy put it this way: "If you prefer to spend all your spare time growing roses or playing with your children, I like you better, but do not complain that you are not being promoted fast enough."[1]

Limiting your job involvement will likely cost you career advancement. But what will not limiting your job involvement cost? Probably time for enjoying God, nature and other people. As Jesus said, "What good is it for a man to gain the whole world, yet forfeit his soul?" (Mk 8:36)

But even if you can't rise to corporate president without completely devoting yourself to your career, can you still make the most of your work opportunities? Tom Peters, one of today's most highly regarded authorities on the subject of business management, and his coauthor Nancy Austin do not think so:

We are frequently asked if it is possible to "have it all"—a full and satisfying personal life and a full and satisfying, hardworking, professional one. Our answer is: No. The price of excellence is time, energy, attention and focus, at the very same time that energy, attention and focus could have gone toward enjoying your daughter's soccer game. Excellence is a high cost item.[2]

I am unconvinced. God has created us so we work most productively when we take time away from work to be rejuvenated.

126

Take Leonardo Da Vinci, for example. The Encyclopedia Americana describes him as "artist and scientist, master of the arts of painting, sculpture and architecture, accomplished engineer, and pioneer investigator in the natural sciences. The most versatile genius of the Renaissance."

The fact that he was a genius doesn't mean Da Vinci accomplished all that he did without effort. He once remarked that "God sells us all things at the price of labor." He did not, however, work constantly. "Every now and then go away, have a little relaxation," he advised. "For when you come back to your work, your judgment will be surer, since to remain constantly at work, you lose power of judgment. Go some distance away because then the work appears smaller, and more of it can be taken in at a glance, and a lack of harmony or proportion is more readily seen."

You may decide you can't succeed at the career you enjoy without putting work before everything else. Even so, God still calls you to put relationships with him and with others first. If you don't, you're bound to become less than he intends you to be. As Lily Tomlin has said, "The trouble with the rat race is, even if you win, you're still a rat."

For Individuals or Groups

1. Is it wrong to be a workaholic? Why or why not?
2. Do you think being a workaholic indicates a spiritual problem? Explain.
3. Pages 123-25 list four indicators of when we are working too hard. In which area are you most likely to be guilty of overwork? Why?
4. Two indicators of when we are not working hard enough are noted on pages 125-26. When are you most likely not to be diligent enough on this job?
5. How do you think your career or your results on this job might suffer if you reduced your work level?
6. Tom Peters and Nancy Austin say in *A Passion for Excellence*, "We are frequently asked if it is possible to 'have it all'—a full and satisfying personal life and a full and satisfying, hard-working, professional one. Our answer is:

No" (p. 126). Do you agree? Why or why not?

7. Da Vinci advised "a little relaxation" every now and then (p. 127). How can this benefit your work life as well as your personal life?

8. What are the barriers you face in getting your work load under control? What first step can you take to overcome one of those barriers?

12

Changing Careers

• • • • • • • •

*C*hange can be exciting or threatening. The bigger the
change, the more excited or threatened we feel.

Entering a new vocation is one of the biggest changes you
will probably ever make. If you are not seeking a vocational
change at the moment, you may see no reason to concern yourself about the matter. But to encourage those who are facing an
imminent career change and to alert those who are not, consider
this—eighty per cent of us switch careers sooner or later. At
least that's what Richard Nelson Bolles claims in his popular and
helpful job-hunter's manual entitled *What Color Is Your Parachute?*:

The job-hunting gamble poses particular difficulties for

anyone who is trying to change careers—as four out of five of us will do, before our lifetime is over. (Remember, even a homemaker who decides to find a job "downtown" is by definition changing careers: from "homemaker" to "whatever.")[1]

Reasons to Consider a New Vocation

Why do so many people embark on new career tracks? Many reasons. Some career changes happen to us. Others we make happen.

Situations that might force you to change vocations include:

☐ becoming physically disabled
☐ being replaced by new technology
☐ working in a saturated or economically depressed job market
☐ being blacklisted
☐ finding yourself unable to make a living wage in your field

Reasons you might initiate change include:

☐ becoming disenchanted with your work
☐ desiring a new challenge
☐ facing new family situations (such as divorce, death of a spouse or children leaving home)
☐ feeling pressure to make moral compromises in your present career
☐ wanting to avoid threats to your health

Let's look a little closer at career changes that happen to us.

Changing Vocations Because You Must

If you're forced to make a vocational change, you need courage to believe good things lie ahead. Courage like Anna Robertson's.

Anna, who grew up on a farm, married a farmer and raised ten children. At age sixty-seven, when her husband died, she took over the farm herself. Farming was all she knew. But in her seventies Anna began to find farm work too hard and reluctantly gave it up.

After a lifetime of working she didn't want to sit idle. So at age seventy-eight, Anna began to paint in oils, resuming an interest in art she had as a girl. The next year an art collector saw her paintings, liked them and bought several. After that Anna Mary Robertson Moses, who became better known as Grandma Moses, painted one thousand pictures before her death in 1961 at 101 years of age.

Grandma Moses, of course, was not forced to make a vocational change until she was well beyond retirement age. In contrast, Oliver Heaviside, who became a telegraph operator at eighteen, learned he was going deaf soon afterward. Six years later he had to give up telegraphy because he couldn't hear well enough to continue.

Oliver Heaviside felt washed up at the early age of twenty-four. But in reality he was just getting started. For the next fifty-one years Oliver researched electric current and, among other things, greatly improved the quality of long-distance telephone communication. As a researcher, Oliver enjoyed many advantages he would never have known as a telegrapher and made a significant contribution to all of us who "reach out and touch someone" via long distance.

If you are facing an unplanned vocational change, take heart. Look to God, your loving Father, to transform your loss into gain.

Help for Displaced Workers

I have cited the examples of Grandma Moses and Oliver Heaviside because we can see their whole lives in perspective. Difficult circumstances actually opened exciting new doors for them.

Today displaced workers enjoy advantages that those of earlier generations lacked. Take Bill Leverenz, for example.

While working as a maintenance man at a bakery, Bill fell and severely injured his knee. The doctor told him that the knee would never be completely right again and that he should seek work that would not keep him on his feet all day. But Bill made good money at the bakery (and hated job hunting), so he stayed where he was.

Bill was also manic-depressive, subject to cycles of extreme mood swings from exhilaration to deep depression. In Bill's case the cycles were long. He would feel high for months and even years, and then low for similar periods.

During an especially difficult period when further knee trouble exacerbated his already severe depression, Bill not only lost his job at the bakery, but his home. Shortly thereafter his wife and three children left him as well.

Today Bill holds a good job in the office of a Christian publisher. How did he bounce back?

"I'm blessed to live at a time when people in situations like mine can find help," he says. "First of all, I can now keep my manic-depressive condition under control with prescribed medication. Secondly, after I lost my job at the bakery I found help through vocational rehabilitation. The people in vocational rehabilitation were ministers of God to me, though they may not all be Christians. I don't know where I would be today without them—maybe not even alive."

Vocational rehabilitation counselors arranged for Bill to attend a community college and earn a degree in accounting. Other agencies then helped place him in a job and get re-established as a productive member of society.

"Nobody will or can do everything for you," Bill says. Some people, too bitter to think of future possibilities, wash out of the vocational rehabilitation program quickly. But Bill found that as long as he tried to help himself, the agencies did what they could to help him.

If you can no longer work at your previous job, check out the services that state, county, city and privately funded organizations make available. There is vocational rehabilitation for the physically disabled, retraining for those whose jobs have been eliminated by technology, and placement agencies for those who lack job-hunting skills.

One of the most comprehensive programs is offered under the federal Job Training Partnership Act. If you are unemployed or underemployed, find out which local agency administers the JTPA program. (Often the local agency will be called the Private Industry Council.) Under this program you can get retraining, rehabilitation, job placement and vocational guidance (with special help if you're under twenty-one or over fifty-five). Sometimes JTPA programs even provide tools, uniforms and transportation to the job.

One more note of encouragement: Under some federal programs, employers get special tax breaks—or even cash subsidies—when they hire hard-to-place workers.

For older workers, counsel and assistance in finding jobs is sometimes available through local colleges, church associations or private agencies. In addition, the American Association of Retired Persons (AARP) operates a Senior Employment Program. The service assists low-income persons fifty-five years or older to obtain paid on-the-job training in community service agencies who simultaneously help their workers locate permanent jobs.

Changing Vocations Because You Want To

As traumatic as a forced career change may be, at least the decision to move is made for you. When you're debating whether to initiate a career change, however, that first step can be tough. First you need to examine what bearing, if any, your faith will have on your choices. As a Christian, should you learn to be content with the job you have? Is your present job a calling from God which you should stick out—or should you aspire to something better?

Not many Christians today consider their occupations a divine calling from which they dare not depart. However, some do. One friend of mine stayed for years in a job she hated because she believed God required it of her. That viewpoint, followed consistently, would create a situation too much like India's now-rejected caste system for my comfort. Supposedly one's station in life is divinely ordained and one is therefore locked into it.

Most Christians who view vocations as divine calling do not press the concept to the point of completely forbidding vocational change, though they may discourage it.

For example, in his book on work and leisure, Leland Ryken writes:

The picture that emerges from the Bible is that God arranged society in such a way that there are farmers, housewives, hunters, soldiers, kings, chariot drivers, and dye makers. His providence, moreover, leads people into one or another of these. If they are not callings from God, what are they?

Ryken says a little later:

The original Protestants saw something else in the idea of calling that may not sit well with a society that conceives of work mainly in economic terms and that lives with images of upward mobility based on job changes in its mind. I happen to think the Reformers and Puritans were right. At the very least we should hear them out.

Calvin, for example, wrote this about 1 Corinthians 7:20: "Each should be content with his calling and persist in it, and not be eager to change to something else. . . . [Paul] wishes to correct the thoughtless eagerness which impels some to change their situation without any proper reason. . . . He condemns the restlessness which prevents individuals from remaining contentedly as they are."[2]

Note that Calvin does not forbid changing vocations, but he does oppose a "thoughtless eagerness" to do so "without any proper reason."

While some people generally display a "thoughtless eagerness" to change vocations, others show too much reluctance to do so. In hard times especially, a play-it-safe mentality leads many people to stay with vocations that really do not suit them.

Paul's point when he wrote the above words to the Corinthians was that they should not change their status in life simply on the basis of their Christian conversion. They shouldn't marry or end a marriage (see 1 Cor 7:8-16), seek to become circumcised or uncircumcised (vv. 17-19) or throw off or enter into slavery (vv. 20-24). They could serve Christ in any of those states as surely as they could out of them.

Because slavery was then a vocation, the admonitions about it especially relate to our discussion about career changes: "Were you a slave when you were called? Don't let it trouble you—although if you can gain your freedom, do so" (v. 21). I believe that last phrase—"if you can gain your freedom, do so" —quite clearly speaks to the question of vocational change today. We could interpret the principle involved as follows: Are you stuck in an undesirable work situation? Don't let that destroy you. Do your work as unto the Lord and he will accept it fully. But if you can better yourself, by all means do so.

Making the Change

As suggested earlier, just changing jobs, let alone careers, can be traumatic. Here are some questions you should ask yourself before taking the plunge into something new.

1. *Are you cut out for the kind of vocation you are considering?* That is, are you going to be good at this new career— and are you going to like it? Those two elements don't necessarily go together.

Craig Selness practices law in San Jose, California. When I first met Craig, he was a promising young minister. He had excelled in his theological studies, and many who knew him were sure he would become an outstanding pastor. Craig could preach, teach and counsel effectively.

When he got into the ministry, however, Craig found important things about it that he didn't like. For one thing, he missed the intellectual and spiritual challenge of relating to people who did not share his faith in Christ. In college, his faith had thrived against opposition. Craig also did not like feeling "on duty" all the time. Though he enjoyed being with people, his privacy mattered to him. Sometimes he wanted to be just another member of the flock, not its leader.

Other elements of the ministry didn't fit Craig's personality, either. He could not find an outlet in church work for his desire to compete. He could, perhaps, have competed to become the largest church in town, but he believed that Christians are all members of one body and that for him to compete with other churches for members would displease the Lord. He also chafed under the open-ended nature of his work. Ministry is an ongoing

136

service that more often than not seems unfinished. He was helping people to grow and to work through their difficulties, but he rarely enjoyed a sense of closure.

For all of these reasons, Craig decided to pursue law. As an attorney he regularly mingles with those who do not share his faith, competes freely with other lawyers in court and experiences a sense of closure at the end of each case. He also continues as an active member and teacher in his local church.

2. *Do you know enough about the vocation you are considering to make an intelligent choice?* After you examine your own skills and preferences, take a hard look at the vocation you are considering. Have you romanticized it? Quitting a job to embark on a career you really know little about can spell disaster.

Although you can read about a prospective career, nothing beats getting firsthand experience. Why not volunteer or work part-time in a job where you can get a more realistic picture of your intended career?

Roberta Hegland knew when she was growing up in the 1950s that she wanted to be a nurse. Caring for the sick (and, in the process, telling them about Christ) sounded wonderful. Roberta read every nurse novel she could lay her hands on.

At age sixteen Roberta became a volunteer nurses' aide. But her dream of becoming a nurse soon began to recede in the light of reality. Most of the nurses were not the compassionate people she wanted to be, and she understood why. To deal with so many suffering people, a nurse must either detach herself emotionally or suffer along with her patients. Roberta didn't feel comfortable with either option. She also realized that she would not have as many opportunities to share her faith as she had imagined there would be.

Roberta's career interests then turned toward helping juvenile delinquents as a probation officer. She hoped to encourage teenagers to turn from a life of crime to a life of productivity—and, perhaps, to Christ himself. As a college freshman she began preparing for a career in law enforcement by studying psychology and sociology. She also began to work as a volunteer at juvenile hall.

Again, Roberta learned that the work did not live up to her expectations. Each officer carried such an overload of cases that individual offenders got little personal attention. Given those conditions, the probation officers did not expect much change in the young offenders. Roberta was also disappointed to learn that probation officers worked under strict guidelines which severely limited their freedom to speak openly about their faith.

Eventually Roberta decided to work with young people at an inner-city church. She and her husband also take foster children into their home. Direct experience with two prospective careers saved her from entering fields she now believes she would have found frustrating.

If you can't gain direct experience, perhaps you could conduct interviews with several people in your prospective field. Don't ask general questions such as, "Do you like the job?" What someone else likes may not be what you would like. Ask questions that reveal what the work actually involves, especially those elements of the job that you expect to be most (and least) attractive to you.

Your questions might include: What variety of tasks does the job involve? How does the job challenge you? Will I make an adequate living in this field or be expected to make financial sacrifices? Will I work directly with other people? What opportunities for advancement exist? How do high-level positions in the field differ from entry-level positions?

Professional Career Guidance

In addition to conducting your own research, you may want to seek professional guidance. The non-profit Johnson O'Conner Research Foundation, for instance, can test your aptitudes and coordinate the results with an appropriate occupation. This organization, founded in 1922, serves clients in Atlanta, Boston, Chicago, Dallas/Ft. Worth, Denver, Houston, Los Angeles, New Orleans, New York, Philadelphia, San Diego, San Francisco, Seattle, Tulsa and Washington D.C. Their testing program takes three half-days and, at this writing, costs $390. They have saved many people a lot of time, trouble and false starts.

John Bradley of Portland, Oregon, operates a career guidance service called The Idak Group. He also affirms the need to take a comprehensive inventory of your gifts and interests before pursuing a given career. To get clients thinking, Bradley sometimes draws three circles arranged in a triangle and overlapping slightly at one point. One circle represents what you like to do. A second circle represents what you do well. The third circle represents available opportunities. At the point where all three circles overlap lies the work you should pursue.

For further help sorting through a career change, I recommend reading *What Color Is Your Parachute?* the practical job-hunters manual I quoted at the beginning of the chapter. It's crammed full of valuable information that's updated every year.

The Career Change that Fails

My son-in-law Bill was a mail carrier for the post office when he first married our daughter Krystal. The post office offered security and good wages, but Bill aspired to more.

I heartily approved when Bill used his GI benefits to pursue a master's degree in counseling. His going back to school meant the family would have to scrimp for a while, but it also promised a brighter future.

Two years later, Bill graduated with his master's degree. He applied for various job openings in his new field and soon landed a position as a family counselor for Grant County in the State of Washington.

He lasted there just less than two years. If he hadn't quit, Bill believes he would have suffered complete burnout. All day long he was dealing with especially difficult cases sent to him by the county. Because many of his clients didn't want to be there, progress in most cases ranged from painfully slow to nil. Worse yet, he was earning less than he did as a mail carrier.

Bill investigated and discovered he could return to the post office. He hated the idea of giving up on his new career and ending right back where he started. But he consoled himself that it would not have to be permanent. Right now he needed time away from counseling. Later, if he could counsel in private practice and not have this continual parade of hard cases, he could make a success of it yet.

Over the next several years Bill gradually realized that pursuing a counseling practice was something he thought he should do because he had gotten the training, not something he really wanted to do.

Bill began to explore other possibilities—including the opportunities for advancement within the postal system. He soon discovered that his training and experience in counseling gave him a big advantage in qualifying for a management position. Just as his training had already helped him in being a better husband, father and Sunday-school teacher, it has now made him a better manager too.

It's not the career he once had in mind, but it's not bad either.

It Will Work Out

As we come to the end of this brief book, I direct you again to Proverbs 3:5-6: "Trust in the LORD with all your heart and lean not on your own understanding; in all your ways acknowledge him, and he will make your paths straight."

As you fully acknowledge and trust in the Lord, you can depend on him to guide you in your vocational choices. For a few people, career goals may unfold according to a master plan they brainstormed in high school or college. Most of us, like Bill, experience twists, turns, disappointments and dashed hopes—but also courage reborn.

In the end, our vocations may look very different from what we envisioned. As the writer of Proverbs observed, "Many are the plans in a man's heart, but it is the LORD's purpose that prevails" (19:21). For trusting children of a wise and loving heavenly Father, that's more than good enough.

For Individuals or Groups

1. What different careers or jobs have you had? What was involved in switching from one to another?

2. Why is making such a change often threatening? What often makes it exciting?

3. A variety of reasons for making a change are listed on page 130. What are some good reasons and what are some bad reasons for changing jobs?

4. As the chapter points out, sometimes we are forced to make a job change (pp. 130-33). What can help ease the transition at such times?

5. If as Christians we are to learn to be content in our present situation, when might it be appropriate to seek a job change?

6. How can you tell if a job is part of your calling or not?

7. Several factors should be kept in mind as you consider a change. Some are mentioned on pages 136-39. What other questions would be helpful to ask?

8. As you think back over this book, what has helped you to take your job and love it?

Notes

Chapter 2
[1]Augustus Neander, *General History of the Christian Religion and Church* (Boston: Crocker and Brewster, 1851), vol. 4, p. 274.

Chapter 3
[1]Walter Henrichsen, *Disciples Are Made—Not Born* (Wheaton, Ill.: Victor Books, 1974), p.153.

Chapter 4
[1]Bill Peterson, "Nine to Five," *Eternity*, December 1984.

Chapter 7
[1]Stanley Baldwin, *A True View of You* (Ventura, Cal.: Regal, 1982). Now out of print but available for $5 postpaid from SBM Inc., P.O. Box 101, Oregon City, OR 97045.

Chapter 8
[1]John Naisbitt, *Reinventing the Corporation* (New York: Warner, 1985), p. 5.
[2]Cheryl Forbes, *Imagination* (Portland: Multnomah, 1986), p. 99.
[3]Ibid., p. 119.

Chapter 10
[1]Hans Selye, *Stress Without Distress* (Philadelphia: Lippincott, 1974), p. 96.
[2]Ibid., pp. 82-83.
[3]Susan Seliger, *Stop Killing Yourself* (New York: Putnam, 1984), p. 53.

[4]Hans Selye, *Stress Without Distress* (Philadelphia: Lippincott, 1974), p. 99.
[5]Ibid., p. 84.
[6]Ibid., p. 97.
[7]Ibid., pp. 64-65.
[8]Ibid., pp. 74-76.
[9]Ibid., pp. 76-77.

Chapter 11

[1]David Ogilvy, *Confessions of an Advertising Man* (New York: Athenium, 1980), p. 142.
[2]Thomas J. Peters and Nancy Austin, *A Passion for Excellence* (New York: Random House, 1985), p. 419.

Chapter 12

[1]Richard Nelson Bolles, *What Color Is Your Parachute?* (Berkeley, Cal.: Ten Speed Press, 1985), p. 42.
[2]Leland Ryken, *Work and Leisure in Christian Perspective* (Portland: Multnomah Press, 1988), pp. 141-47.

105301